VOLUME THREE

THE BREAKWATER BOOK OF

CONTEMPORARY NEWFOUNDLAND PLAYS

EDITED BY DENYSE LYNDE

BREAKWATER BOOKS
P.O. Box 2188, St. John's, NL, Canada A1C 6E6
WWW.BREAKWATERBOOKS.COM

PLAYWRIGHTS CANADA PRESS
202-269 Richmond St. W., Toronto, ON, Canada M5V 1X1
WWW.PLAYWRIGHTSCANADA.COM

LIBRARY AND ARCHIVES CANADA CATALOGUING IN PUBLICATION
    The Breakwater book of contemporary Newfoundland plays
/ edited by Denyse Lynde.

ISBN 978-1-55081-636-5 (pbk. : v. 3)

    1. Canadian drama (English)--Newfoundland and Labrador. 2. Canadian drama (English)--21st century. I. Lynde, Denyse C. (Denyse Constance), 1955-, editor II. Title: Contemporary Newfoundland plays. III. Title: Contemporary Newfoundland plays.

PS8315.5.N5B74 2012   C812'.60809718   C2013-908491-6

Cover painting: *Baffin Study: Keel River Valley*, gouache on prepared paper, 2007, by Christine Koch. Courtesy of Christine Koch. www.christinekoch.com.

First edition: May 2016. Printed and bound in Canada by Marquis Book Printing, Montreal.

Breakwater Books and Playwrights Canada Press are committed to choosing papers and materials for our books that help to protect our environment. To this end, this book is printed on a recycled paper that is certified by the Forest Stewardship Council.

We acknowledge the financial support the Government of Newfoundland and Labrador through the Department of Tourism, Culture and Recreation; the Canada Council for the Arts; the Ontario Arts Council (OAC); the Ontario Media Development Corporation; and the Government of Canada through the Canada Book Fund for our publishing activities.

CONTENTS

INTRODUCTION

Playwriting in Newfoundland is a complex and intricate field. These artists know the craft well and delight in pushing the form's limits. They refashion the format constantly. Likewise, genre is reconsidered. They make heavy demands on their physical theatres, their active imaginations stretching the traditional walls of performance spaces, showing time and time again that nothing cannot be asked for. All is made new. Whether it is in the form of a one-person play, a setting in the North Atlantic Ocean now or in 1000 CE, or in two contemporary tales of present-day St. John's, these playwrights introduce us to new and compelling stories and to innovative ways to tell them.

Robert Chafe's *Belly Up* premiered in 2003 at the D.F. Cook Recital Hall at Memorial University in a production by Artistic Fraud of New-foundland. It was remounted in April 2007 at the LSPU Hall and toured to Théâtre La Chapelle in Montreal. It is a one-person performance piece, but it is defined by its ambiguity and complexity like no other. As Chafe writes, "All action and sound in the performance is pre-scored and precisely timed to the soundtrack of a constantly playing back-projected digital video." What happens is the actor, in this case also the playwright, acts against a screen on the back wall. This screen plays what the actor is doing in real time, like a mirror image. It is quite fascinating to watch, though execution must be hell for the actor and crew. The story being told is simple enough. A blind man waits for the return of his mother. But she never appears. Has he been abandoned? What should he do? He waits with his one companion, a goldfish. Then letters begin to be delivered. Yes, letters to a blind man. Here the back screen is not merely the action on stage. It also begins to beat out another rhythm as it introduces other characters and separate action. For example, at the end of the first scene we see a young child with an older woman. She seems to pull him out of water of some kind.

As he struggles alone he increasingly feels isolated. Has his mother merely gone to the grocery store? Where is she? Mail never came and now it does. What does this mean? Just as the letter arrivals accelerate, the play comes to a fitting mini climax as the mailman's name badge flies through the mail slot while the video reveals face after face in a postman's uniform. The mailman's name is Albert. The days pass. No mother comes. The unnamed blind man becomes hungry and the video continues to mirror and enhance his sense of desperation. Images of water abound, and throughout the play the fishbowl sits on the table. We see the blind man when he was thirteen doing public speaking. Is this the subtext? Is this memory? Is this nightmare? In this case, the playwright firmly centres the play on the blind man and his imagination, his memories, his fears, his passions, his sightlessness. The blind man is surrounded by the fish, dead or not, and the apparently menacing postman Albert; Chafe takes the one-man format to a new height. The performer, the video, and text mesh perfectly together.

Andy Jones too uses the one-man format in his play, *Albert*, first produced at the LSPU Hall in St. John's in 1983. While Chafe's play also has an Albert character, and both plays share simple domestic settings with pets, the centrality of mother figures, and characters with an overriding need to leave their homes, these two plays couldn't be more different. Albert and our blind man are set in sharp contrast. In Jones's play, we have Albert sitting at his kitchen table talking to his budgie, Dopple. It is Friday night and he says he is happy because he has all of his work done and has a whole weekend to do whatever he wants. In fact, he is the only one at his office "who is completely up to date." Jones focuses his play on three specific days and although Albert, like Chafe's young man, wants to go out, he will not.

Albert is about one man's dilemma. He is in love with Miss Burnamthorpe, a woman he works with, but he cannot tell her. His reasons are murky. At the beginning he says some things are "True and some things are False." In fact, he ends his Friday night by proclaiming "Maybe I don't even love her!" Following a blackout we see Albert at breakfast with his budgie and he details for us the witch that waits for him every day at home. He tries to see a way out of his problem, and although he wants to go out, he seems unable too. It is on Sunday morning that we discover the source of his dilemma. Promises made by his mother to the Witch Who Could Not Get Enough Love haunt him, and although he finds he loves this creature, he likewise hates her. Therein lies his curse. While Chafe uses video extensively, almost creating another character, Jones has his character act out all, from what he sees as his little dirty joke to the pain he lives with, and has Albert jumping in and out of his story and finally singing and shrieking his way through his tale. At the end, however, Albert does find some degree of contentment with his lot.

Berni Stapleton looks to the water for her play, *A Rum for the Money*. It was first produced in 2007 by Theatre Newfoundland Labrador. In the North Atlantic we find three men in the *Miss Tillie*, a dory with a small outboard motor. On board we meet twenty-year-old Jim, forty-year-old Frank, and sixty-year-old Jack. After the dramatic opening in the dark when we hear men running and shouting and the sound of rifle shots, we realize the three have just escaped the Saint Pierre police. They have been rum-running, or, as Stapleton puts it, taking part in the "original smugglers' market." On the surface the play is about three smugglers, but it revels in exploring the lives of these men behind the caper. As the opening chase recedes from memory, they relax. The men talk and laugh, but always keep an eye out for a patrolling Mountie cutter. We get to know them well and we care about them. We learn about their very different plans for the money they will make from their take.

As they share a flask, fog begins to move in. Non-swimmer Jim relaxes and decides to have a smoke and offers one to the others. They scream at him and throw the lighted match into the water. Anything can reveal them to the searching cutter. As the fog gets thicker they are joined by whales and Jack reminisces about seeing a mermaid. But then Jack hears something on the water. Not only does he hear something, he sees a huge vessel bearing down on them. No longer is it enough to have the play staged *on* the North Atlantic, Stapleton pushes further. She has a blackout and "we hear the splintering sound of *Miss Tillie* being torn asunder." The opening of Act Two is grim. With heavy fog it is difficult to see, but we hear Jim screaming. Jim, alone in the boat, is trying to haul Frank in. The vulnerability of the men in this tiny craft is fully realized here. With Jack apparently drowned, it is the two men we watch and feel for. They support and cajole each other in order to keep their spirits up. However, we begin to despair for these wet, freezing smugglers in their broken boat. Precisely at this point, Stapleton shifts the action effectively and effortlessly to bring the play to a satisfying conclusion. Here the uncaring North Atlantic is the villain that must be acknowledged and respected.

The water of the North Atlantic is also prominent in Aiden Flynn's play *The Monk*, which was first performed at the Rabbittown Theatre in April 2010. However, Flynn's focus is a little different. He turns to a much earlier period, 1000 CE, in an unspecified outport from where the Norse explored the North Atlantic. Specifically we have a Norse settlement where the chieftain's wife has brought a Christian monk to convert the village. The man, simply known as Monk, has built a small Christian chapel, and at the play's opening he is cleaning up after a service. This monk, however, is only human, and although no food is to be eaten in the chapel, he can't resist a piece of cake. With his mouth full and a guilty look on his face, he receives a man at the door. Quickly it is established that this other man is not here for worship. He is the one man from the community who has not joined the new church, but he is clearly curious. The two men discover they have a lot in common. The old man, Grenjar, admires the workmanship of the building and asks if the monk built it. He had. The young monk says he has heard that Grenjar is a boat builder. He is. Finally Grenjar accepts the offer of a chair and the two men share their pasts. The old man does tell the monk that he thinks his new religion is merely a fad and the old religion will withstand. This assessment is made without heat and the two men part without acrimony.

The second scene opens in Grenjar's boatshed where he is working on a knarr, a Viking boat. As he works he appears distracted and cuts his hand. This opening is reminiscent of the monk's behaviour at the beginning of the first scene. Of course at this point Monk knocks on the door. First refused entry, he is finally allowed in and he says he has come to hear about the Norse gods. He also offers to suture Grenjar's hand while they talk. They discuss both religious worlds and their beliefs and as Monk leaves he says he came "to see your chapel, I guess," and another bond is made between these two contemplative men. Here the vast North Atlantic Ocean has a different character; it is an open highway on one hand, and an essential part of religion on the other. Grenjar's knarr is to be part of his funeral, his funeral pyre. It will be transformed into an essential tool, leading to new life travelling the endless waters.

The contemporary world of St. John's is depicted in *Hail*, a two-act play first produced in 2011 at LSPU Hall. Playwright Edward Riche is also a screenwriter, radio writer, and novelist and is clearly comfortable in all forms. He has three other plays, each sharing his strong satiric voice. In

Hail, four men meet to discuss the possible ramifications of a crime they committed when they were much younger. It is apparent that the men, now fathers and senior partners, first knew each other at university. During their university years, these four, plus a fifth man, stole a considerable amount of money from the institution. Now it appears that the fifth, Lionel, is being questioned by the police. Why, no one knows, but speculation and imaginations run wild. Gerry and Len are the first to appear. They meet at Paul's garage as arranged and wait for Paul, who has gone to pick up Danny for their meeting. Not surprisingly, violence erupts as each man considers personal costs. Even from the outset it is clear Riche has created four very different and complex characters.

Act One lays out the possible consequences and tensions run high. Len is the first to lose it and turns on Paul. With his hands on Paul's neck, he truly appears to try to kill him. Gerry and Danny finally pull Len off Paul. As all the men try to calm down, Danny starts to shake, throws up on himself and collapses. Once they get Danny lying down and more comfortable the act closes as Paul heads out to see if Lionel is home from the police station. Act Two begins with Len and Gerry talking while Danny rests. Soon Paul returns with the news he has spoken to Lionel's wife. While he found nothing of substance the men each find their own interpretation of her parting words, that "all will soon be known." Their conclusions are characteristic. Paul believes that an apology will suffice. Len thinks that they can all run away and form new identities. But it is street-smart Danny who tells them how they can truly "become" someone else. Each man separately ponders what he will do when what they believe is the inevitable actually occurs. Alas, they still do not know why Lionel is being questioned by the police and when their cellphones start ringing from an unknown number, their uncertainly grows. In Riche's confident hands, the conclusion is brisk and satisfying.

Also set in contemporary St. John's, Lisa Moore's *February* tells a very different tale. First produced in 2012 by Trinity's Rising Tide Theatre and based on her award-winning novel of the same name, Moore's play recounts the poignant story of Helen O'Mara and her son, John, whose husband and father, Cal, perished in the *Ocean Ranger* tragedy. The play, like the novel, delicately moves back and forth from that awful February night and before to the struggles of the now-adult John and Helen's own steps towards finding a new life. The play strikingly begins with John and Helen in separate spotlights as they remember how father/husband died. The separate light suggests that they are isolated—and they are—but truly they are not. They are individuals intertwined and Moore makes this clear by careful, almost musical, word repetition and select unison lines. Scene two deepens the separation but oneness as we find Helen awakened by a phone call from her son in a Singapore airport. This scene begins with cacophony of sounds—of a storm at sea, radio static, alarm bells, planes, church bells, and into the ringing phone—and it is this sound montage that reflects the very structure of the play.

February is about that fateful Valentine's Day but also about a widow and son. Moore has carefully intertwined the two stories, the two lives. These stories are often mirrored with actions and even repeating words, phrases, sentences. Helen's pre-marital sex that results in conceiving John is set against his own supposed one-night-stand with Jane and her subsequent pregnancy; actions and words echo. Words also echo beyond the two tales. Helen's words from the first scene are echoed in scene seven when an unknown driver helps the grieving widow back into her house after returning from Pier 17 where the bodies were laid out. Further, the scene of Helen giving birth to her youngest daughter is mirrored by Jane's labour with John's daughter. Likewise the climactic scene physically and verbally links the sinking of the *Ocean Ranger* and Cal with John's failure of a safety course, which includes a simulated helicopter in a swimming pool. Echoes and mirrors abound in the very structure of the play as we begin and close with mother and son on two chairs separate but together.

The art of playwriting in Newfoundland is flourishing, but it is still a complex and diverse world. *Belly Up* and *Albert*, the two one-person plays collected here, could not be more different. The physical theatre's walls are pushed and stretched. One extensively uses video while the other relies entirely on performance. Likewise, the focus on boats by Stapleton and Flynn are similar but remarkably different. For Stapleton, the boat is her setting and the men are physically adrift. For Flynn, the boat becomes the actual funeral pyre. Contemporary St. John's is shared by Riche and Moore, but how it is created and used is contrasted once again. For Riche it is a solitary night in a garage where his characters must consider past actions. For Moore it is the backdrop of a fateful February night, but it is also the years before and the years after. Each play places special demands on production. Video, water, or performance creates clear challenges but for these playwrights the resulting plays are stimulating.

Many hands have helped me bring this volume together. Of course, the playwrights have all professionally responded to my questions or queries. Throughout the entire editing period I have had the assistance of, first,

Francesca Boschetti and, subsequently, Alley Waterman, graduate students. Of course, I remain indebted to the publishers, Breakwater Books and Playwrights Canada Press, and their staff.

— DENYSE LYNDE

BELLY UP

BY ROBERT CHAFE

For Mom

NOTES ON SETTING, TEXT, AND PRODUCTION

The action of the play takes place in the foyer-cum-dining room of the hero's house. There is a rectangular dining table centre stage, and behind it a large gilt-framed mirror (more on that later). Downstage left there is a small bench seat, and upstage right a hung window covered by a venetian blind. Upstage left there are several full garbage bags, some open. The physical set is all greyscale, and other than these set pieces the stage should be empty, the playing space sliding off into darkness on all sides.

Belly Up utilizes music and digital video to achieve many of its goals. All action and sound in the performance is pre-scored and precisely timed to the soundtrack of a constantly playing back-projected digital video, projected onto the gilt-framed "mirror" centre stage. The video begins by projecting a mirror image of the room and the performer. When the performer is facing the audience the video (a mirror) behind him shows us his back and, literally, the fourth wall and its accompanying door. In the mirror image the room is detailed and in vibrant colour, as opposed to its physical stage counterpart. The images projected occasionally diverge from the physical and present the character's fantasies and fears. The mirror effect is possible because of the precise scoring of stage text, blocking, and gesture with the video's soundtrack and thus the video's text, blocking, and gesture.

In the script it should be assumed that at any given time images on the screen are the mirror image of the present stage action. At times when this is not the case screen images are denoted in the stage directions in **bold**.

Belly Up premiered in 2003 at the D.F. Cook Recital Hall at Memorial University in St. John's, in a production by Artistic Fraud of Newfoundland. It was remounted in April 2007 at the LSPU Hall and toured to Théâtre La Chapelle in Montreal.

Performer: Robert Chafe

Director: Jillian Keiley
Stage manager: Jeff Baggs
Product manager: Erin French
Technical director: Flora Planchat
Rehearsal assistant: Mark Bath
Film director: Lori Clarke
Film producer: Ann Connors
Musical theme composer: Petrina Bromley
Music and music arrangement: Lori Clarke
Set and prop design: Shelley Cornick
Costume design: Karen Rehner
Video and stage lighting design: Flora Planchat
Cinematographer: Nigel Markham
Film first AD: Paul Pope
Underwater camera assistant: Baptiste Neis
Editing and animation: Chris Darlington
Production assistants: Tiffany Martin and Liv Groenningsather
Script breakdown: Kelly Stone
Film performance stage manager: Danielle Irvine
Film performance assistant stage manager: Mike Worthman
Swimming coach: Jennifer Adams
Musicians: Don Ellis, Lori Clarke, Petrina Bromley, Shelley Neville, and Matthew March

ADDITIONAL FILM PERFORMANCES

Terri Andrews, Evan Bursey, Bruce Brenton, Jason Card, Pat Flynn, Barry Buckle, Dale Jarvis, Delf Hohmann, Dick Buehler, Dick Stoker, Paul Pope, Russell Bowers, Bobby Hall, Mike Hikey, Neil Butler, Steve Cochrane, Mike Worthman, Geoff Hann, Jeremy Eaton, Don Ellis, Duncan Finlayson, Martin Weinstein, Jason Brophy, and Roger Sampson.

1

In the darkness... footsteps and counting.

One, two, three, four, five, six. Six steps. No. Six, seven, eight. And one half turn.

Beat.

Dark, eh? Man walking in darkness. So you can't see the shine off my nose. Or the cheap pyjamas. Or maybe I'm naked. Maybe just so you can't see the look of terror on my...

Beat.

When I did public speaking, in junior high, I would always look for a kind face. Oh well.

Beat.

Enough already. Turn up the lights. Good luck. Yes, because this, this is not the kind of darkness from which one can emerge. This, this is the kind of darkness one walks into. This, this is what I "see." No! Yes. Since age ten, total darkness.

Beat.

Boo hoo.

Beat.

They say the other senses are strengthened. To compensate. And they are partially correct. I still can't tell Coke from Pepsi, but my house, our house, was always crystal clear. Pieced together from twenty years of finger tracing and counted footsteps.

Beat.

I can still see my home. But now, from memory. I can see the simple wooden table...

Lights up on the table. He stands downstage in the shadows, silhouetted.

...bevelled edges, deep wood grain, forgive me but I don't know the colour, and the one chair...

Lights up on the chair.

…simple, flat back, where I sat every morning at nine, eating my waffles and pulp-free orange juice. I can see the table and the lone weight bearing on it…

Lights up on a cloth-covered object in the centre of the table.

…covered in its cloth now. Shhh. That means he's sleeping. I can see the bench…

Lights up on the bench.

…wooden, with cloth seat, next to the door, where Mother would sit upon her return from shopping, removing her boots and reading the mail she collected from the post office as she's done for ten years. Ten years from the post office, no home delivery as the noise of the mail slot would give her a start. I can see the mirror my mother bought to make the room look bigger.

Lights up on the edges of the mirror.

I can see the gilded frame of the mirror, though after age ten its reflections were a mystery. A mystery, so I would dream myself inside that gilded frame. Me and my world, in brilliant color. The terrible talent of imagination.

*The mirror lights up **a colourful fourth wall, and a single door with a mail slot**.*

And I can see a door. But nothing beyond it. Everything outside of it, outside the familiar. Unknown. Terrifying. Darkness. And that… I only ever walked out into that darkness two years ago. Two years ago. And there is someone outside that door.

Lights quickly fade up on him. He stands in the centre facing the door and us. There is an apprehensive pause.

Well, you can come in.

Pause.

I'm not going to be angry.

Pause.

I mean I should be. I could be angry. Very angry. But I—I realized, over the last little while I've realized, that to be angry here, to be angry in situations like this, would be to be ungrateful, and I realized that I am—I am very grateful. I am.

Pause.

So. You can come in. I'm not angry.

Pause.

I was. Perhaps I was a little angry. Before. At lunch. Dinner. And the next dinner. And breakfasts. Definitely at the breakfasts. I was very very angry at breakfast. Admittedly. But, not anymore. I am very grateful. For everything, and I—I realized that there must be a very good reason, a very good reason because you are considerate. Yes, you are considerate. So. I'm sorry I was angry. That was wrong. I know that there must have been a very good reason. And here you are and everything is fine and I am apologizing for doubting you. For being angry.

Pause.

So. You can come in now.

Pause.

I don't know what else to do but apologize. I mean. It's not like I shouted at you, or gave you a hard time.

Pause.

I couldn't. You weren't here.

Pause.

(shouts) I didn't shout at you! So what? What are you waiting for? Are you waiting for complete panic? Because we are close. We are very close.

Pause.

(softly) There has been no one to talk to. No one, and, and you know, you know how I like to talk.

Pause.

So you can come in. Please?

Pause.

Mother?

*There is the sound of a cuckoo clock, and then a loud whoosh **as a letter slips in through the mail slot and falls incredibly slowly to the floor. As it lands** there is a room-shaking boom. He leaps back. Footsteps are heard walking away. Pause.*

Oh, my.

Blackout.

A mournful aria begins as black slides slowly to deep blue and lighter blue, shimmering and out of focus. Credits begin to roll as the image solidifies to an underwater view. Light trickles down from above, dancing around us. A long, peaceful view, and then, suddenly, something at the bottom of the frame. The hand of a young child listlessly floats into our view, and then his arm. The music crescendoes and the surface is broken by an older woman's arm and hand, which fiercely grabs the boy's wrist and yanks his body past us and quickly up and out of frame as the aria hits its highest note. The screen goes black. The aria abruptly ends.

A pause.

2

*Spotlight up on him sitting in the chair in the middle of the room. His eyes are closed, lost in thought, dreaming. **The screen is black.** There is a silent pause. He slowly opens his eyes. As he does so, lights come up on the rest of the stage, **and the screen illuminates to a mirror view of the room.** Another small pause.*

We don't get mail.

He handles a black envelope, feels its edges.

But, I am open to new things. I am.

He faces the door.

I am open to new things, and I am not going to be—to get discouraged by this. We are not going to get discouraged by this. So. Let's get on with it.

A pause. He drops the envelope to the floor and speaks immediately.

I'm not going to open it. Certainly. I think that's fitting. Some person, some mailman, and that's an assumption, drops something through our door and I am just supposed to… to…

He points at it accusingly.

The potential here is staggering, and disturbing!

He steps away from the envelope. A tense silence.

I don't care what it has to say or ask or report because, because it probably has something to say, something important to say, but I don't care, I really don't because the potential is staggering and quite possibly disturbing and we don't even get mail, and I can't read the bloody thing anyway!

A small pause. He continues, more calmly.

And while I have many many questions, many questions, I don't need the answers, I don't need them, really, I don't really need anything, anything else because, because, even given the circumstances of my life, I am happy. Really. Right now in this moment. I'm delighted. And I don't need to be thrown a bone, or a… a… thing with the rope and the… I don't need it. So.

He continues to face the letter.

You hungry? I'm hungry.

He turns to face the object on the table.

'Cause even though it hasn't been nice, 'cause it hasn't, I haven't told you everything, I really haven't, but it hasn't been nice and I guess I owe you an explanation, but sometimes I just don't want to talk and sometimes I don't even think you are listening. I am happy. That's true. I am happy, and I don't need… anything, because, because I have a home, a safe home. And I have my mom. And I have a good friend. Even though he doesn't listen.

He walks to the object on the table.

You awake?

He takes the cloth off a small fishbowl. It is filled with opaque, black water.

Mom's going to feel bad about this. When she gets home. That is true. That… is what is true.

He picks up a small container of fish food next to the bowl and shakes some into his palm, which he then tips into the bowl. Pause.

You are hungry, aren't you?

Pause and a smile.

And you are listening.

He stands over the bowl, his hand gently on its top edge circling.

3

He hears a noise approaching from outside.

Garbage day.

He listens to the truck outside.

Maybe I could throw it out the window. But I would never reach the street, and if you, if you should hit someone then you're, you'd be the worst in the world.

Pause.

I could scream. Something. Fore, or something. Timber. It would be their own fault. People walk with their heads down.

Pause.

It's smelly in here. Eh? You smell that?

Pause.

God it does smell though, eh?

A sound behind the door.

Hello?

Pause.

Hello? Mother?

A letter slips through the door. *He hears it and makes a speedy decision.*

Wait. Wait please!

He immediately regrets his decision and stands in silence for a second facing the door. He makes another decision.

Ah, hmm, look. I, ah, I need to talk to you. And this, this is not an invitation to come in, okay? Ah, God. No, no, under no circumstances should you consider this an invitation to come in. I, hmm, but I just need to talk to you. Hello? Okay? Are you still there? I think you are. You are, aren't you. Yeah. Anyway. I just want to say that, that what you heard yesterday was a mistake.

He reacts to his own choice of words.

Misunderstanding, ah. Look, you, ah, you see, I thought you were my mother, and we, well we have this game we play when she comes home that I am mad at her and that I'm hungry and angry and she stands at the door and—look, anyway, look, point being that. Yes. Everything is just fine. Really. Really. Everything is fine. In case you were wondering everything is just fine. I don't need anything. I tell you this because you should really not consider this an issue, this door, this voice, you should not consider this an issue at all, in your travels. Nothing is wrong here. So, don't go calling... people. Okay? Okay?

Pause.

Hello?

Pause.

Don't go calling people. No footsteps. Which means. Either you are gone. Or you are... not. Not. If not, why not?

He listens. A very long pause of silence.

You're gone. You are gone. Did you hear any of that? I don't need help!

Pause. He leans his forehead against the wall.

I need novelty. I need something new here.

A figure cloaked in black darts across the room. *He swings around, grabs the chair, and shifts it in front of him. He listens.*

That. That's not funny. That's not funny.

Pause. His breath deepens.

Hello?

Pause.

No, I'm not doing that. There is nobody here.

Pause. He listens to the quiet and motionless room.

I'm just tired. Too tired to be up.

He waits a second, his eyes darting, and then he walks quickly away from the chair.

4

Later that day. He stands by the window. The screen shows a perfect mirror image of the room, except for the chair that he had moved. The mirror shows it in its original position.

Up until four days ago I'd never spent a night alone.

Pause.

I realize that I'm being selfish here, that I am only thinking of myself. I mean Mom does not do well in the world, either, you know. And I am worried, but at least she knows where the hell she is. And where the hell I am. I mean, I'm not going anywhere.

Pause.

And the coincidence is not lost on me, the fact that, the fact that she does not come home from a very elementary trip to the grocery store, and, let's face it, it is, it is elementary, and two days later, two days, and we're getting mail. We don't get mail!

Pause.

The coincidence is not lost on me.

Pause.

If they are from her, well that's, this is all a, a pretty sick joke.

Pause.

And if they are about her...

Pause.

A pretty sick joke. Because at the very least I feel, I feel I deserve an explanation. If nothing else. For the years of unending mysteries, this, this just being the latest, like buying a mirror for a guy that hasn't seen his hair in years, or like giving me a glass bowl that might as well be, be lead with a pet that I can't even... pet. I'm blind, Mom! Or did you fail to notice. What, did you think I just didn't like eye contact? Sure, don't come home, send a letter. Why don't you just saran-wrap the toilet, or set off the fire alarm. Why don't you spin me round real quick, hand me a knife, blade first. Why don't you...

*He walks towards the bowl and hits the chair. He stops suddenly. **The chair immediately is where it should be, against the front of his legs.** But he is disoriented. He turns his head confusedly.*

5

*Lights up on the next morning. The cuckoo sounds **and the mail slot loudly opens. A letter is poked through and about to be dropped when he speaks.***

I don't live alone.

The letter pokes through the slot, unreleased by its holder, trembling ever so slightly.

So, I don't know what you think you are up to, okay? There are people coming and going here all the time. This place is a zoo, honestly, so, don't expect discretion, or anything, because whatever you think you are doing, or plan to do, will be on the six o'clock news, okay.

A small pause. The letter is finally released and falls to the floor.

I don't know what these are. You hear me? I don't know what these are. These letters. I won't open them. You can keep pushing them in here and I won't open them. You hear me?

A pause.

I want you to stop delivering these. Can you do that? Can you stop delivering these? Actually why don't you just stop everything. I would like you to stop coming here, and standing around. I would very much like—I would like a new mailman. I'm making a formal request. Because, quite frankly, sir, I think what you have been doing is a little, well I'm gonna say it, it's been a little unusual. And unnerving, it's true. So I'm making a formal request. I do not want you as my mailman any longer. Now. I suppose that will do it, or do, or do I have to make it official, put it in writing or something. Is there someone I can call? Did you here me? Is there someone I can call? The post office? The post office I imagine. I'm gonna call the post office and lodge a complaint. I'm going to do that and you have no one to blame but yourself. Because you have been unusual. I'm going to call and lodge a complaint. At the post office. I'm going to need your badge number, or something, I don't know if you have badges, I just don't remember, but I'm gonna need it. Your badge number, or your name and title or something. I'm gonna need your name.

Pause.

I'm gonna lodge a complaint.

Pause.

I want a new postman.

Pause.

I'm picking up the phone. I'm dialing.

Pause.

Please. Just go away. Please.

A small object flies through the slot. There are footsteps away. He looks at the door awhile in silence and then very slowly makes his way to and finds the object, and picks it up. He feels its surface without looking at it. He speaks.

Al… Alb… Albert?

The door opens and immediately there is a fast progression of people, as through we were flicking through a Rolodex looking for one in particular. All wear a postman's uniform. Some smile happily, others grimace. Some beautiful, some hideous and frightening. The progression eventually grinds to a halt on the face of an almost humorously handsome man in his twenties with a cheeky smile. Albert stares and smiles at us for a moment, and then tips his hat. His teeth gleam. The door closes and we quickly zoom out to mirror image. He stands with the name badge in his hand, still facing the door. He manages a small smile.

6

Later that day, late afternoon. The sun cuts long across the room. He leans on the table looking at the door. A big breath.

Grocery day.

Pause.

Her absence is going beyond annoying to downright… inconvenient.

Pause.

I hate this. This waiting.

Pause.

There was a time. Believe you me there was a time when I could be doing something about all of... this, all this.

Pause.

I'm hungry. I'm not ashamed to say that. I'm very hungry, even though I'm at an age where... I should be, I should be doing something about all of this. No. No, not where I pictured myself at this age.

Pause.

I'm hungry. It's a basic human need. Food. The basic human need, really. I mean, what else is there? Sleep. It's been five days now. I'm none the worse for wear.

A nervous giggle. Pause.

Affection. Maybe. Maybe, affection. Okay, affection, affection, yes. I do need affection; we do need affection. Of a sort. Perhaps of a sort. But one has to, one has to be very careful with affection. It demands a tremendous amount of trust, it is, it can be, a black hole, it can suck everything else away if you get too close.

Pause.

I have done that. I have relinquished all spirit and movement to others. Call it a fault. Amidst my many more wonderful traits lies, it is true, the ability to be a putz.

Pause.

There was a time when I could be doing something about this. And there was a time when I did relinquish all spirit, it's true, freely and willingly. Though sparingly. Very sparingly. And she was quite special. She was a special one. Oh, she could make me feeble. She could wipe away any streak, any stain of gumption. And I'm like, here, take it, take it all, because she's just so... great.

Pause.

Mother never met her, and that's probably for the best, but I can't help but think she would agree. I mean this one, this one earned my trust with her eyes, yeah? And wasn't that something.

Pause.

Not now. Not anymore. Back then, I suppose, with my healthy awareness, and my healthy eyes, I could sift through the good the bad and the ugly just by looking at them, but now, now it would just be like squeezing fruit. You could only tell so much, about the peel, and as for what's going on inside, as for the rest of it, you would just have to leave it up to luck. Or faith.

Pause.

Hmmm. Fruit.

There is a low rumble through the room. He is startled; he scans for its source. There is a slightly louder rumble. He is concerned. There is a third rumble, very loud. The room tremors as though there's an earthquake. Pictures fall off the walls. It eventually stops and settles. He realizes its source. He looks to and touches his belly. A small massage and a blank look.

I need food.

Albert bursts through the door with armfuls of groceries that he promptly drops on the floor at his feet. Albert smiles big and tips his hat. Albert and the groceries disappear. A small pause. He looks at the door.

7

It is the next morning. A letter through the slot. He doesn't hesitate.

Thank you.

He speaks quietly to himself.

So.

Deep breath. Forced bravery.

So. It's been a long time since I've met anybody new. It's, ah, difficult, you know, getting out. My schedule is so busy these days, it's so busy that it's hard to find the time. Even for the little things, you know. Errands. I find I—well, I find the day just, it flies by. It flies by, and before you know it you've worked it away, worked it all away, and you haven't even gotten out to, know you, pay the bills, and such, or to, say, buy groceries. For example. Because I don't get out too much. Because... I'm very busy. And it is very rarely that I meet somebody new. Like yourself. So. It is very nice to meet you, Albert. Someone like you, to ask a favour, should I need. And vice versa, of course. Someone with whom to share histories. To have in for tea.

The cuckoo sounds. He immediately realizes and regrets what he has said and he retreats from the door to the edge of the room. He paces silently. He struggles to recover.

Someone to. Uh, histories. I used to be a public speaker, uh public speaking. I did, I did a, an aptitude test. You know, those tests in elementary school, the ones they never let you see, but your parents, your mother can see if they really kick up a stink, and, well, Mom, my mother, she can kick up a stink better than, than, well, anybody, and it said, the test said, that I would be a good politician, among other things, because of my great skills in reasoning, among other things, and the principal said that the only things, one of the things, that would hold me back was, uh, my shyness, because I had somehow, somewhere along the way become very, well, shy, and that was, that was not always the case, and, and well the next thing I know I am public-speaking.

*He walks to centre, almost seeing the audience. **He walks to centre stage. He is thirteen and wearing a baby-blue polyester suit. He is led by an older woman, a teacher.***

And I was terrified, I was, but my friend—I had a friend. Her name was Cathy. And she. She told me that when I got up, to talk, publicly, that I should first thing, before opening my mouth, before saying a word, I should look for a kind face. Notwithstanding the sheer numbers in the audience and notwithstanding the noise of the room, look for a kind face, and then all the others, the disapproving, the angry, the dangerous, then all these faces will seem that less important.

Pause.

So that's what I used to do. Look for a kind face. And I would always find Cathy. Except when she was sick. Which was often on account of her bladder problems. And on those days, bladder days, I would just look and look and look. And. I don't know.

He looks up to the door again. He takes a deep breath.

Sometimes the universe offers up the one person you need, just when you need them.

A pause.

Have you ever done public-speaking? Or anything? Albert? Albert?

A small, silent nod.

8

He is on his hands and knees feeling his way, searching.

I've never really taken a good look around, you know, ever since I
couldn't look, but I mean mother was never really the type to throw anything out, anything that wouldn't rot, you know. I mean I wouldn't call
her a pack rat but she liked her things. My things. So who knows what's
poked away in here. She still has my old blue suit.

Beat.

You wouldn't know, your needs being few, what—a few glass pebbles,
a plastic tree—really, but these things, these little things, can be a great
source of comfort, and who knows what she has poked away in here. And
where. God I loved that suit. Maybe my lunch tin, with the Muppets.
And my Donny and Marie dolls with the little plastic, the little micro-
phones that stuck through their hands. And my, my old nose plug.

Beat. He stops feeling around.

My nose plug. I almost forgot about… The stuff we keep. Who needs it.
Better she did throw it out. Why dwell.

He stands up.

Pointless really. With my luck she hasn't kept any of it, anything, and if
she did I wouldn't find it, and if I found it I would end up regretting it
because you look for one thing and you can't help but finding trouble,
finding trouble, with my luck.

He looks towards the door.

His name is Albert. I think I had an uncle named Albert. It's a nice
name, you think?

Beat. He looks towards the bowl.

I'm not trying to make friends. That is not my intention here. I just
think. I just think it would be good to be able to have someone to… ask,
to ask if things get bad. If things get worse. But they won't. They are not
going to get worse, and I rationally know that, it's just precautionary.

Beat.

Besides, he's a mailman. Who's ever heard of a dangerous mailman?

Pause. The door opens to reveal Albert. He tips his hat and smiles. A beat, and then he is suddenly cloaked in black cloth as he hoists a heavy chainsaw into frame and rips its cord. His face drops into a sadistic sneer. And then, just as suddenly, everything returns to normal. A closed door and an empty room. Small pause.

I won't talk to him again. I promise.

9

Lights up and it is night. He stands beside the window and fingers the blinds. A pause.

I don't like this. I don't like this having a window. I really don't.

Pause.

I've honestly lost all interest in what is out there. And sure it would be nice to be able to have someone to talk to. No offence. To talk back. I know that people are too much trouble, generally. Generally, loud and, and aggressive, and warm to the touch, yes, but cold, cold and deceptive, very deceptive, and not easily, not easy to... People. Searching for their better half. Like salamanders looking for a lost tail. They don't see it. They, them out there. They would tell you this is a cave. They would tell you that we are hiding. But they don't see what I see. They don't see it.

Pause. He faces the bowl. He walks to it and traces his finger across the surface of the water.

Of all the things we grew to hate, water was the last. We were at the pool.

Underwater scene as at the top. Ripples and shafts of light from above.

I wasn't going to school, anymore. I rarely went out, as I was getting worse, and the world was getting no better. It was a Tuesday morning, I remember that, and there was no one there, and it was warm.

A boy's hand drifts into frame.

And it was... sublime. And... comfortable. Like sleep. And like most everything else...

A woman's hand reaches in and pulls the boy by the wrist. We return to a mirror view. Pause.

We went home, and never talked about it again. She gave up the last little bit of herself that day. It was the last little bit she really showed me.

Pause.

Mother was a synchronized swimmer, don't you know. Very good, apparently, in her day. Competed all across the country. I told her once that I wanted to give it a try, take lessons or something, and she just laughed because, well, I'm a boy. And, anyway, you can't sync what you can't see.

Pause.

She has a history. And she has had her reasons. I may be in the dark, but she has had her reasons.

Pause.

Some things we know, some will be revealed. Some we may never know. But. We will not become hysterical.

A black cloaked figure lurches across the room. They stop with their back to us and begin to turn. We are about to see their face. And then the room is empty. His breathing is thick, laboured. He is white as a sheet.

I am truly. Being. Haunted.

10

Lights up for morning. He stands over the bowl. A long pause as he stares at the fish. The cuckoo sounds. ***A letter flies through the door.*** *He stares at the door. A shadow lingers. A pause.*

I suppose you think I didn't call the post office. I suppose you think that I, as soon as you gave me your name, I would change my mind, that you would give yourself a face in my head and that I would feel bad about reporting you. I suppose you think that I consider you my friend now. I suppose you are waiting to know my name, and I suppose you expect me to tell you. Well guess again, because I still think that this, all this, is unusual, a lot more unusual than it need be, and if you think that I'm gonna give out my name to somebody, just because they happen to be my mailman, just because they happen to deliver my mail, my personal mail, my… my personally… addressed…

Pause.

I suppose you think your clever now. I suppose you think that this is funny.

Pause.

I didn't report you. But. But I can't talk to you either.

Pause.

Go away please.

Pause.

Look, you could be anybody, and just because your name is Albert, that, that doesn't exactly narrow it down, you know. You could be crazy. You could be. You could be a danger to yourself and others. Do you own a van? You could. You could own a van, and not a mail van, not a harmless mail van. You could own a big black van. A big black van with tinted windows. You could've cruised the neighbourhood, neighbourhoods full of children. I know your type. I wasn't allowed to walk home alone from school because of your type. Walking home with Mom because the big black van was spotted the day before circling the corner store. And we knew what you used to do. You used to have the big old sliding doors on the side. You had the big old sliding doors on the side and you'd pull up next to a kid, a single kid, only when they travelled by themselves, and drag them in, and then bam, they were gone, and no one would hear anything about them ever again. And it only used to happen when there was a single kid, and it only happened to kids visiting from out of town for a while. Well… well that's because they… they never knew anybody well enough to… to walk with them. So they were always alone. Look, the point being, I know your type! Murderer!

Pause.

Do you? Own a van?

Pause.

I don't know, Albert. I don't know. I've thought about this, this little phe-nomenon we have going. Don't think I haven't.

Pause

It's against my better judgment, but.

Pause.

I find it hard to believe that you are a murderer. If for no other reason than the fact that I'm still alive.

11

Lights up for morning. He is standing above the bowl. He shakes the fish-food container over his hand. Nothing. He tries again. Nothing. Long pause. In a sudden burst of anger he throws the container across the room. An embarrassed and thoughtful pause.

I'm sorry. I'm sorry. I do feel emotion, and I do have emotions. Very real emotions for you. This will be okay because, because it is always okay, and even though this looks bad, much worse than it has been, it is going to be okay because, because we have each other, yes we have each other and that, that is a very powerful thing. Don't you underestimate it, don't you forget and underestimate this, the value of this. This love.

Pause. He has caught himself off-guard. He backs away from the bowl.

I have used the word before.

Pause.

Mother and I never used the language. But it is important to remember that it is there. That the word is there. When you need it.

Pause.

You think I'm not capable of that, in any real way? Not capable of real affection.

Pause.

You think I couldn't be married? That I couldn't make that commitment? That I couldn't love a woman, a beautiful woman, because she loved me too. She loved me, notwithstanding my difficulties. And because we share things, common things, like a, an affinity for poodles, and barbecued pork. And that we couldn't have a kennel in the backyard, where we would raise puppies, for sale, and, and supplement our income, and that she would sing me to sleep. And we would have friends in for tea and buttered scones. Because they are her favourite, and because she loves people and she instills the same, that same trait in others. We would have friends in for tea and scones. Notwithstanding the weather. Before it got dark.

Pause.

And she would leave her scent in the room. So that I never, never really felt her absence. Even when she was long gone.

Pause.

I have used the word before. And it does not burn me. As I have been warned.

Pause. He walks to the bowl.

I do... care.

Pause.

Point being, I do care. And. And, because of that, you must believe that... it is going to be fine. And you must believe that it is going to be well. And you must... that...

Pause.

I'm sorry.

Pause.

I'm just... as hungry... as you. Just as tired. And. I'm sorry.

A pause.

You hear?

He gives a sad smile and slowly walks away from the bowl.

No.

He looks at the door. He stands and traces the hands of the cuckoo clock with his fingers. He looks at the door again, and makes a decision. He walks quickly out through his hallway door and after a beat returns with an old garment bag covered in dust.

It would only be right to dress well, to make a first impression. He comes every day at three. Mother always said punctuality was a sign of a person who thought kindly of others. But then again... Mother was always late.

Beat.

I know what you're thinking but... I can't go out there alone and... I'm just as hungry as you are. And food doesn't grow on trees. Well... trees don't grow in here.

He shakes the dust off the garment bag and opens it. He removes a black suit **(baby blue suit)** *and lays it on the table next to the bowl. He gives a look* *towards the door and then begins to put on the shirt. He picks up the hanger to remove the jacket and the cuckoo clock sounds. He pauses and looks up to the door expectantly, listening. There is silence. There is no mail. He comes to a realization and in slow and silent shock drops the hanger with the suit to the floor behind the table. He takes a silent pause, leans on the table, and collects himself. He bends down behind the table to pick up the suit. Lights out.*

12

The lights are still out on stage. A time-lapse in the mirror. He emerges from behind the table with the suit. He puts it back in its garment bag and walks it out into the hallway from where he had retrieved it. He returns. A series of activities in time-lapse, through daylight and into night, that build to a climax of frustration and panic, and end in a short blackout.

13

The blackout lasts long enough for the cuckoo to sound. Lights back up in the mirror and on stage. He stands motionless, staring at the door. No mail. Behind, the time-lapse, still in effect, betrays him. He starts moving once again throughout the room: a series of activities that build to a climax and then end with him in his stage position. The time-lapse ends.

14

The cuckoo sounds. No mail. A long pause.

Mother would never let me use pennies.

Pause.

She would never let me use any currency under a quarter. She was well-read in diseases of the day.

Pause.

She would wretch. Literally, she would wretch. A kid buying a bag of potato chips and then, with not so much as a rinse, dunk their infected little paws into ketchup powder and suck it off. And see. Should his tongue fall off, should he poop out his stomach, everyone would be oh, oh how tragic, how cruel, how senseless, oh oh, but there, there in that bag of ketchup chips and palm of mouldy pennies, there… is… the cause. Lack of caution.

Pause.

Nothing less than a quarter. 'Cause, otherwise, the monetary value, it's just not worth the risk.

Pause.

Point being, Mother is well aware of risk, and was every time she stepped through that door, so, so I think we can rule out, you know, foolhardiness.

Pause.

And I think it prudent not to run on assumptions here, and go off half-cocked and really panic. Just because she hasn't come home in over a week. And because we are all of a sudden getting mail. Of some kind. And then not. I mean, I always have unanswered questions. Plenty of things I don't know, and won't know, and sure, just because I have panicked in the past doesn't mean I have to, now.

Pause.

Like you, for example. While perhaps not being the best sort of pet for a blind sort of person, you do offer a certain comfort, and as always I am sure Mother had her reasons, but there are many, many things I don't know about you. There is a lot about you that I don't know. Yes, much. Like, like your colour, size, your general appearance for starters. But, just because I can't see you, that doesn't mean that you are dead.

He pauses, silenced by his own words.

No, it…

A pause. And then he races suddenly to the bowl and presses his face to it. A pause.

We have a lot in common. We live, we live by instinct, yes? Ripples, and reflections.

He pulls back from the bowl. A small pause.

But you, oh you are sublime and beautiful and, and the picture of self-respect. And you do not lie. To yourself, or others. And when you do die, you give a delineating sign. You leave no question.

Pause. His fingers trace the top of the water. He stops.

There are plenty of things I don't know. But I am losing... patience.

Pause.

I've never complained. And there has been reason—I have had reason. But I have been obedient. I have listened to her. I have heeded her words, and I trusted when she said that she would... be here, always be here, which is clearly, clearly not the case. It is clearly not the case that she will always be here.

Pause.

You know, when I was a kid I was always terrified. I guess because I had all these notions of all the horrible ways I could die. Car flying off a cliff. Poison. Plane crashes. Big black van. But. It never occurred to me; she never told me. That something could happen. To her.

Pause.

Not once.

Pause.

I have ten answers to every question. And they are all bad. Where are you. What... the hell happened to you, Mother. What the hell is going to happen here.

Pause.

What is going to happen here.

Pause. He stares blankly ahead.

(softly) Here it comes.

15

He leaps into action. He runs to the garbage bags and begins to awkwardly sift through them while he speaks.

I have body fat. I'm lucky for that; she fed me well, and I enjoy a good bread, so I have body fat, and that will sustain me. But after that. After the fat is all gone, and it is going, you don't have to be vain to see that, after the fat is gone, then things take a turn. The body panics, it doesn't quite know what to do—nothing coming in and the furnace needs to be stoked, so it panics.

He finds some old orange peel. He sniffs it and then begins to scrape it against his teeth as he talks.

Starts taking muscle, living meat, to convert to fuel, stripping the arms, the legs, to keep the heart awake. Breaking down its own resources, eating the only tissue that can possibly provide future relief, the breadwinners, breaking them down to keep the furnace stoked. Burning the house to heat the living room.

The room bursts into flame. *He jumps, startled. He turns and faces the door.*

Albert!

16

Lights up on the room. He speaks loudly and feverishly.

Albert?

Pause.

Albert, please, I need food, Albert. I'm in a fix, Albert. And I know I don't know you, well, at all, really, I know that, but. I need... assistance, please. I need food, Albert. I don't have any food and I need food, and I couldn't ask you before, because, because that would mean so many things, so many things, not the least of which, I would have to open the door, Albert; I would have to open the door for you, and I just wouldn't, I just was not able to do that.

Pause. He listens to the silence.

Albert? It's not you, Albert. It's just… I have always found it difficult to believe that someone, anyone, would take an interest. I mean someone who wasn't intending to, to do something bad. That someone would just listen.

Pause.

Albert? Things are grim. Things are becoming grim, Albert, and I'm not left with much choice here, so I need food, and I'm asking you to get me some, because I just can't, I cannot go out there; I cannot go out there, Albert, so I need you to get me some food, and some fish food, some fish food, because I have a fish. I have a fish, Albert.

Pause.

Albert?

Pause.

I bet you have pets too. Yeah? And a family. So, you know, Albert. You know.

Pause.

You never speak to me, Albert. I've noticed that. I've also noticed that you haven't been here in a while. You don't come here anymore, Albert. And I know that there probably isn't any more mail. But I'd be a liar if I didn't say I was a little disappointed.

Pause.

It's been fun. It has. It's kept me alert. Talking to you. And.

Pause.

I don't want to stop. I cannot stop, Albert.

Pause.

Yeah, I bet you have pets. And a family. A big red door and hedges. I bet you walk out that door every morning, run your hands along the hedge. Yeah? I bet you walk at a nice clip. And you smile at people. Sure you do. You smile at all of the people that you know. By name. And they smile back. I bet you drop off your mail quickly. Do your job efficiently. No time to dally. No time to listen at doors. No time to stand and listen. I bet you tell great stories though. Of the few times you did. Slipped your badge through the door. Albert. I bet you name isn't, really—Albert.

Pause.

I think that might be the most disappointing thing, Albert. That you're not even out there. That you won't be coming back.

17

It is early evening. The last traces of the setting sun leak into the room. He sits next to the bowl.

I wish I were like you. You don't even seem to care. You're starving to death and you don't even seem to care.

He begins picking up water in his palm and letting it trickle back into the bowl. He is hungry.

It just wouldn't make sense. It couldn't make sense for both of us to die. Hungry.

His hand comes to rest inside the bowl, and then as though shocked to alertness by what he was about to do, he removes his hand and backs away from the bowl. A pause. He screams at the bowl.

You... are too... dependant on me!

Pause.

And... I am not one... on which to be...

Pause.

I am not one. I cannot do anything to remedy this. This.

He points to the window, the door.

That... is what is killing us. So, you can stop it right now; you can stop laying blame, because I have done what I can.

Pause.

I have done what I can.

Pause.

It's all so ugly. All of that. I think about it and I think, I think there is nothing worse. There can be nothing worse than out there.

Pause.

And, and thinking that. It becomes harder and harder to explain. Explain away this feeling that, that if I don't hear a voice, or hold a hand, or feel that warmth, that certain warmth that only flesh, human flesh, can generate. If I don't feel that...

Pause. He moves to the mirror. He touches it.

She bought this. To make the room, my world, a little bigger. And she gave me you. For company.

He speaks in a genuinely threatening tone.

So don't you dare.

He turns back to the fish. Pause.

She gave me you, because I love to talk, and I love the water. And I loved the pool, and so did she, and I never will know what atrocities were happening around me, that day, every day, what, what made her pull me out, drag me home, never take me back, never talk about it again. I never will know if it was all, if everything, everything was in her head, or if I just... couldn't... see, could not see some real threat, some imminent disaster. I never will know that. But.

Pause.

I have the terrible talent of imagination. I can see so vividly sometimes. What must have happened to her. What will happen to us.

*There is a low rumble. **The room shakes violently.** He slumps against the wall and looks at the ceiling.*

How did you get here? How did you get here—go from... big and blue, and open and, and free. And one day.

Clumps of worms push through the top of the door frame.

When you are hungry. You are so hungry. You fall prey. For the first time, you are more hungry than you are afraid.

A chainsaw comes through the door. Blood seeps under the crack.

I don't... know. I don't know if I, if I am that hungry.

*Pause. **The rooms shakes violently.***

I have a tickle in my stomach.

*He puts his hands on his belly. **Plaster falls from above.***

I have a strange, a tickle in my stomach, but the closest thing I can compare it to was my first day of junior-high public speaking…

The door opens and the walls part once more to reveal a packed audience. A pause. He walks to centre stage. There is a spotlight on him. The young boy in the blue polyester suit is led centre stage again.

…or maybe the first time I spoke to her…

A spotlight on a young woman in the third row. A spotlight on a young woman in the third row.

…the first time I touched her, because I do believe, I know that I did love her, really loved her, and I think it had everything to do with weird little things like her bladder problems, and her love of poodles, and her odd use of the word notwithstanding in every second sentence. And because she made me feel so entirely, entirely, un-alone.

A small pause as he simply smiles at her. Her spotlight goes out. Her spotlight goes out and the walls close once more. His smile does not fade, as his spotlight does.

And though we never married, or raised puppies, or even knew each other after junior high. We could have. I know that we could have.

An axe cuts through the door.

I know that, and I know that she, she is a constant reminder that I can, I am able, also able, to imagine good things, good, beautiful things, things that could have happened.

Another axe cuts through the door.

I could have made happen, let happen, if you had allowed me, if you had seen more than what you… stood to lose. If you hadn't been so afraid. I hold you responsible. I hold you personally responsible for what has happened here, what will happen here.

The door falls from its hinges.

Do you hear that?

A dark figure enters through the door.

I hold you responsible.

The figure begins to walk towards him.

Mother?

Everything returns to normal. The door is on its hinges undamaged. Very quiet. He opens his eyes. The room is empty. There is a pause. Just as he begins to recover the dark figure enters the frame from inside the room. It stops, quite a distance from him, and they just stare at each other. A pause. He is having difficulty catching his breath. The figure removes its hood. A woman's face appears in the soft light. She walks towards him. He lowers his head. He cannot look at her. Her hand extends and barely touches his face as he raises his chin. She slowly retracts her hand from his face and touches his chest, his heart. He reaches up and touches the same place as she retracts her hand. She offers an apologetic smile. She slowly walks off and out of view. He watches her go. His hand still grips his heart where his mother had touched him. He notices something. His hand slowly reaches into his breast pocket. He very slowly retrieves a swimmer's nose plug. A long pause as he looks at it in silence.

I guess we all fall prey.

He puts the nose plug on. He looks back up to where she has departed.

I am also able to imagine good things. You are on a beach. And your hair is wet.

A pause. The room gives a tiny rumble. He smiles and places his hand on his belly. He looks towards the door.

I do have a tickle in my stomach. Where there should be pain. And a, an odd sense of... joy where there should be...

A bigger smile cuts across his face. A long pause. He turns to the fish.

So, maybe. I think, maybe I might know what it's like.

He climbs up on the fish's table. Big smile.

I think you might too. Like if you were swimming. But it was the ocean.

With a deep breath he leaps off the table. A deep, blue ocean, and a figure plunges in feet first. There is a bright flash of blue that mutates quickly into a pervasive and shimmering lighter blue. He is suspended in deep-blue water, traces of bubbles leaking from his mouth. His eyes scan around him and then focus outwards towards us. A hint of a smile. He turns and begins to swim away from us. As he fades in the distance the picture and the room slowly and steadily fade to black.

18

Lights up for morning. He sits on the chair facing the door. He is wearing a blue polyester suit that is far too small for him. The cuckoo sounds. He immediately begins to speak in a chipper tone.

Good afternoon, Albert. Fine, thank you, how are you? I've been having a busy one, not unlike yourself, I'm sure. There is a lot going on in here, Albert, let there be no doubt. You know… how you can, you can let things go. I have been airing the place out. And I have been rolling some coins. Some quarters.

He hoists up a heavy bag and rests it loudly on the table.

Quite a few pennies. And… I have been doing some exploring, going through some old things.

A pause. He puts one of the letters in the pocket of his coat.

The stuff we keep.

He goes to the window and opens the blind for the first time. Beyond the window is impenetrable darkness. He stands as though staring out through it.

It's been impossible, the quiet. My fish is dead. I'm sure he must be.

Pause. He turns and faces the door.

I don't know what these are. These letters, Albert. Why you, all of a sudden, started coming here. But, but I do know… that… sometimes the universe, it just offers up…

He picks up the fishbowl. He very slowly starts to make his way to the door.

Is it nice outside? The weather I mean. The weather is what I'm unsure of.

He extends his arm to open the door. It opens slowly. Beyond the threshold is a wall of darkness.

I'm not afraid of you. If you are there. Even if you're not. I'm not afraid of you, Albert. Not nearly as afraid as I used to be.

He steps through door into darkness. Lights out.

THE END

ALBERT

BY ANDY JONES

For Charlie Tomlinson

ACKNOWLEDGEMENTS

With thanks to Nigel Markham, the LSPU Hall, St. John's, and the Rhu-barb Festival, Toronto.

Albert premiered at the LSPU Hall, St. John's, Newfoundland and Labrador, in 1983 with Charlie Tomlinson as Albert. It was directed by Andy Jones.

CHARACTERS

Albert

SETTING

The kitchen/living room in Albert and his budgie Dopple's tiny bachelor flat.

TIME

Every Friday night, every Saturday, and every Sunday.

ALBERT is seated at the kitchen table; he is humming "Strangers in the Night." Dopple is in a cage on the table; next to the cage are dirty supper dishes and a toaster.

ALBERT: Mmmm Hmmm Hmmm Hmmm Hmmm Mmmm Hmmm Hmmm Hmmm Hmmm. Oh I'm as happy as a bird tonight. Mmmm Hmmm Hmmm Hmmm Hmmm. Happy as a little birdie! Mmmm Hmmm Hmmm Hmmm Hmmm. If I had wings I could fly. "You have a right to be happy, Albert." I know I do, little birdie, because all my accounts are done. I'm the only person in the office who's completely up to date. And now I have the whole weekend ahead of me. I've even had my supper, little birdie...

(not quite so happily humming) Hmm hmm hmm hmm. Oh I'd love to go *out* somewhere this weekend. Out to a bar or something. But I know I'll never do that. No sense thinking about it. I can do anything I want this weekend. I could run naked through the streets.

A little giggle.

Oh my I couldn't do that—I'd be arrested.

Pause. He's picturing himself running with abandon in the street.

Wooooooooooooooo!

Pause.

I could twirl in the streets. No one would mind that. Wooooooooooooooo! No one would mind if I twirled. They might put us away though.

(to Dopple) Then my little birdie'd be in a cage.

He gets the joke. A dirty giggle.

Oh my. If the crowd at the office only knew half what goes through my mind sometimes.

Pause. Sigh.

I like Miss Burnamthorpe. She's so hard and cruel. Sometimes I ache when she stings me with a criticism. *(enjoying the pain)* I just ache for hours.

Pause.

(slightly burdened) The whole weekend. I suppose I could retype my file-heading labels. No—that's going too far. I'll get funny again if I

spend the whole weekend doing that. I wonder what I did that day. No one ever told me. I wonder if I twirled… Oh I'd like to fall asleep now for the whole weekend and dream that… everyone from the office came to visit me or something.

Sigh.

Oh, why don't I just go out? Because I would die, and no one wants to die, little birdie. *That's* why I don't go out. I'm speaking to you now, Miss Burnamthorpe. Out loud. Some things are True and some things are False. And it is true that it is… *(checks the clock)* eight o'clock on a Friday night. And I miss you and I am thinking about you. I can't wait for Monday morning. I am living with a Witch who won't let me talk to anyone but her.

(in ghost-story mode) If I tell anyone about her she can hear me and she will turn my heart to ice!!!

He drops in and out of story mode as he continues.

The part about the Witch is false, Miss Burnamthorpe… *(back in story mode)* She will turn my heart to ice so that I will no longer be able to ache for you! You see the bind I'm in, Miss Burnamthorpe. This is false what I am saying now. The only truth is, and I'll say it again: it is… eight… *(checks the clock)* thirty on a Friday night and I miss you and I am thinking about you… Once a year the Witch loses her magic powers. On that day I could tell you. But that day always falls during my summer vacation. And what if it turned out that you loved me? The next day you'd speak to me, the Witch would hear, and my heart would turn to ice. What a day it would be though, Miss Burnamthorpe!

"Why, Albert, I thought you were on vacation."

And then I'd tell her directly.

(to Dopple) Would it be better for us to tell all and lose everything the next day?

"But, Albert, if we never mention it after today perhaps the Witch won't find out…"

You don't know the Witch, Miss Burnamthorpe! And besides, we'd have to wait another whole year before… or… maybe she wouldn't love me but at least I would have told her and I could *ache* for the rest of my life. What is wrong with me.

He checks the clock.

It's ten o'clock. Oh my. If I'm not careful I'll get funny. I should do some exercises.

(in ghostly voice) Miss Burnamthorooorpe. Calling Misss Burnamthorpeeeeee. I loooooooooooovvvvveee yoooouuuuuuuuuuuuuuuuu.

Pause.

Maybe I don't even love her. The bars will be closed in half an hour. Thank God. Because then I... can... go... to bed!

Blackout.

Lights up; it is Saturday morning.

The table is neatly set. ALBERT *lights a candle. He fussily arranges everything on the table. He sees a crumb, picks it up, brings it to the garbage, then sits down.*

(to Dopple) Brek, breks!

He pulls Dopple's food lever.

(either) Didn't you hear there's a ban on chirping? *(or)* Is there a ban on chirping?

He talks to the bird a bit, then suddenly jumps right back into story mode.

Every night when I come home the Witch is waiting for me. I'm so frightened in the front porch, I can hear her low laugh. Hahahahahahahaha.

It is a frightening laugh; his eyes widen with real fear, yet he likes this sound.

Oh.

He shakes himself out of it.

She sits there staring at me with her dead eyes. She is the most beautiful creature in the world... *(melodramatically)* but her eyes are dead!!! She watches me make supper and she laughs all the time. Hahahahahahahaha. Because she knows all the bad things inside of me—everything, the deepest shame and embarrassment. Then she takes me to bed, and then she kisses me with her dead lips, and I just lie there; I cannot move. For even though she is more beautiful than you...

Pause. He thinks, but does not know where to go with the story.

…She smells funny. Dead. She hasn't… gone off or anything. It's more like she was flash-frozen the moment she died. Then she brings in a party of dead men and devils and she tells them that I hate her, and I tell all the dead people that I don't, and to prove it I kiss her. Then she pushes me away and says that I love someone else, and I almost, almost, almost, almost, almost tell her about you. I want to confess, Miss Burnamthorpe. She makes me feel sorry for her, but because it is the one thing that she does not know about me I don't tell her.

Pause.

I'll bet that no one in the office suspects I've just spent the night with dead men and devils.

(to Dopple while pulling food lever) Sup, sups!

ALBERT *plays with the birdseed. His head snaps up and in a computer-type voice he says:*

I am now gone funny.

ALBERT *sings.*

I'm thinking of youuuuuuu, Miss Burnamthorpe, Miss Burnamthorpe, you you you you you you… yeah!!!

This is an opera. There must be some magical way that our hero can escape from the Witch, or some god that he can call upon to release him into your arms.

Pause. He realizes there is a problem with this thought.

But if he thinks about it will the Witch be able to tell? No!

(improvising) That's another thing the Witch can't do; she can't tell when I'm thinking of ways to get rid of her.

He presses the toaster lever down.

"But where is the Witch now?" asks Miss Burnhamthorpe on the Toaster Transmitter.

Speaking down the toast slots.

She's visiting her mother for the weekend.

ALBERT *seems to see something. He goes very still and quiet. He is almost afraid for himself. He stands up, looks for escape, but there is none. He's alone.*

Oh my, I should go out, I should go out, I should.

He blows out the candle.

Blackout.

Lights up; it is Sunday morning.

As the lights come up Albert removes the birdcage cover and plays with Dopple. Then he goes to his armchair and continues the story.

Once upon a time many years ago, long before even I was born, and I am a very ooooooooold man, there was a man and a woman who got married and they had three sons and they called them Tom, Bill, and... Albert. Now, Tom and Bill withered at birth, and when Albert was born he began to wither too, but he was pulled back from the brink by a man called Foot. Foot Frye was his name, a very, very fat man who sold used toothbrushes and second-hand paperback books door to door. This man saved Albert byyyyyy... means of... *(making it up on the spot)* the three promises! Promise number one: Albert's mother had to promise that she would die by her own hand at the age of forty-two; promise number two: Albert had to promise to live with the Witch Who Could Not Get Enough Love; promise number three...

Pause. He cannot think of another promise.

...will only be revealed at the end of the story. And so Albert did not wither away and he grew to be strong and well, though somewhat thin... but, boys and girls, his mother was another story. For as soon as the promise was made to Foot Frye she began to grow weaker and weaker and weaker and weaker. Doctors and priests were called in, as well as a few sensible people; they came from all over the world, and the doctors went away cured of their own diseases, but unable to cure Mother. A doctor with a club foot danced away; a blind psychiatrist became a world-class archer; a very proper, though barren, English missionary doctor became pregnant shortly after returning to her African clinic hut. Fourteen priests went away with their sense of humour restored but unable to cure Mother. A number of dyed-in-the-wool sensible people, the type who speak plain and true, will not put up with any nonsense, kick-in-the-pants school of natural psychology types, they were called in too. But they all left shaken. Some turned to drink, some actually cried in their beer, but they were unable to cure Mother. Books were read, alternative people from the west coast of the land were consulted, but there was no doubt that Mother had decided to take her own life slowly, over a period of years, by means of staying indoors, not getting any exercise, and by eating a shocking amount of ice cream and chocolate… At forty-two she seized up in her rocking chair and was laid to rest. It was a cold night, the snow was white, the trees were black, and there was Albert, sitting at the side of his mother's grave, shaking with the cold, and so as not to go mad—holding back his sobs (of which there were a surprising number left). Aching, Miss Burnamthorpe, aching… when all of a sudden a dog began to moan, the moon increased in wattage, and a pale figure was… *there*. No Poof! No Bang! Just… there… "You must be the Witch," said Albert, as cool as a cucumber. Yes, Miss Burnamthorpe, it was she, the Witch Who Could Not Get Enough Love, and around her head flew a hundred *horrible* devils! There was a fearsome beating of black wings and… *(afterthought)* they had the weirdest chins in Christendom, rats' tails on the end of them! Hundreds and hundreds of years passed—at least it seemed that way to Albert—but it was only a handful of human years and Albert found that he loved the Witch, much to his surprise, needless to say. In spite of himself he loved her more and more every day. When he wanted to talk to his dead mother the Witch could take on her shape and manner… almost… and he could have a pretty decent conversation. At least a lot better than most people can have with their dear departed ones… The Witch became the friends that he was no longer able to have—for the Witch forbade it—and I must say, all in all, she did a legion job on that score. The Witch became all things to him, and he could not help but love her. But the Witch was unsatisfied. Some nights she would shriek and conjure up her devils EEEEEEEEEEEEEIIIIIIIO-OOOOOOOEEEEE!

He shrieks in an unearthly manner. He is frightening himself but enjoying it.

And through her beautiful lips she would whisper in a demon voice:

"You will betray me and love someone else… I know it. If you declare your love for another I will turn your heart to ice, then you will feel for no one else ever again."

At that moment he hated the beautiful Witch and loved her at the same time. "Why can I not love someone else? This is truly my curse," said Albert to himself.

And then one day, Albert went funny, and it was because of his summer vacation. Every year he spent his summer vacation keeping his accounts up to date, catching up on old work, relabelling old files. He had to, you see; he had to because he was afraid; he was afraid that in the relaxed atmosphere of holiday time he might meet a potential love or friend, and declare his love, thus turning his anxious heart to ice. But this particular year he worked far too hard, and he went funny. Nonono, not like I'm going funny now, not a weekend funny, but *funny* funny. After two weeks of accounting, filing, labelling, his conscious mind grew wings and flew the coop... and while on its flight his mind stopped in to visit his two brothers, Bill and Tom, the very two brothers who had withered at birth. Bill and Tom had only lived in the world a couple of days and were therefore very very very very very foolish boys. "Albert"... they said to him, "Why don't you..." Get this now... "Why don't you... declare your love for Miss Burnamthorpe and..." Get this now... "Just. See. What. Happens!!!" Bill and Tom were just out for a lark, never having lived in the real world. But at the end of the two-month funny period they convinced Albert's mind to go for it, so his mind flew back to the coop and said to itself... "Stop acting funny, stop being a crazy person, and they will let you out of here and you will then have the opportunity to declare your love for Miss Burnamthorpe!" But on his way back to the office he stopped in to see the Witch... da da da da!!! Well to make a long story short, the Witch was suspicious when Albert returned and she said, "Oh, by the way, if you should happen to declare your love for another it will kill me." And then she took down the book of current curses and there it was, as large as life, curse number 4,568,904, the Witch who cannot get enough... *(picking out key words from the imagined book)* Who Cannot Get Enough... when Albert declares... she... dead. Yes, boys and girls, dead in the funeral home, yet-another-elephant-struck-down-by-a-poacher-in-darkest-Africa sense of the word. D-E-A-D. Dead! "Albert," said the Witch, "Say goodbye to the mother in me, the friend in me, et cetera. When you kill me you kill them too. When your mother died you couldn't do anything about it. Oh oh oh how you wished you could do something about it. Do you remember?" "Yes," replied Albert. "And now," said the Witch, "you have the opportunity to stop the death of your new mother, your new friend, et cetera."

Now, boys and girls, do you remember at the beginning of our story I told you that there was something that I would tell you later on? Am I right, or am I wrong? For I am a very ooooold man. Speak through the Toaster Transmitter, Miss Burnamthorpe!

He depresses the toaster lever and listens. Nothing.

Does anyone in our audience remember?

He waits until someone in the audience says "the third promise."

Right, right!!! The third promise!!!! The third promise made by Albert on the day of his birth falls into two parts. Part A—that Albert would never knowingly kill or cause to be killed any other human being, witch, wizard, warlock, fairy, or troll, whether through war, through neglect, or through the course of justice as we know it. And part B—that if he did so, at the very moment of that person's, witch's, wizard's, warlock's, fairy's, or troll's death, his mother would begin an eternity of torment in the land of Twalla (where people go while awaiting final sentencing by the great powers)—isn't it incredible, boys and girls? Isn't it incredible? That this reality should exist side by side with Albert's burning love for Miss Burnamthorpe? But that's life, boys and girls. *That is life!*

Needless to say Albert never said anything to Miss Burnamthorpe, and he never ever went *funny* funny again.

He only loves the Witch sporadically now. Mostly he just lies there and gets kissed. Sometimes he hates her, but she doesn't seem to notice… after all she could never be loved enough anyway.

Pause.

And now the weekend is almost over. The bars will be closed in a little while. Our hero is not too badly off. He has a beautiful Witch who kisses him every night; he lives in fear of the demons that attend her. More exciting perhaps than the life of the average suburban dweller. But, of course, this is all false. That I ache for Miss Burnamthorpe is true. But let us suppose that tomorrow at ten past nine I go into the office and I say "I love you" and she says that she loves me. There is a courtship, a disappointing love life… I've lost my solitude, my bird. I see the children as hers. Hate them. Hate her children; the children grow in a loveless home… I begin to ache for somebody new; I talk to someone else on the Toaster Transmitter, but I cannot declare my love for them, for my heart would turn to ice, it would kill Miss Burnamthorpe, and banish my mother to Twalla forever, and that is the solemn vow made on the day of my birth… and besides… I promised.

Blackout.

THE END

A RUM FOR THE MONEY

BY BERNI STAPLETON

PLAYWRIGHT'S NOTES

One particular rum-runner was especially reluctant to speak with me when I was researching this play. He was long retired (yes, retired with all the dignity and trappings of any other career-minded individual) but still worried about wiretaps, narcs, and snitches. We talked about his experiences as a smuggler during the fifties and sixties and he bemoaned the fact that in these modern times all the skill and artistry had been lost. It was this conversation that prompted me to hone in on the fifties and sixties in my play, rather than trying to encapsulate a broader, more sociological examination. For, as we spoke together over tea and bickies in his immaculate kitchen, I came to believe that his worry about wiretaps and the like was really only a way to remain validated. In fact, no one cared any longer about him or what tidbits of knowledge and capers undiscovered he still kept. My thanks to the Grand Bank Regional Theatre, to the Resource Centre for the Arts, and to Theatre Newfoundland Labrador for their roles in the development of the script, and my eternal gratitude to Jeff Pitcher, who validates us all with his work and craft.

This play was researched using confidential sources. Dramatic licence has been taken in order to protect identities. All names have been changed.

"Rock of Ages" was written in 1776 by Augustus Toplady as he huddled under a rocky overhang seeking shelter from a storm in Cheddar Gorge, England. It is said he wrote the lyrics on a playing card. It was set to music in 1830 by Thomas Hastings.

"Jack Was Every Inch a Sailor" is a Newfoundland folk song.

PUNCTUATION NOTES

A forward slash (/) in dialogue or mid-dialogue indicates that the actors should speak over one another or juxtapose their dialogue.

WORDS OR SLANG

Sove: a slang for the past tense of "to save."
Fetch: a "fetch" is a spirit or harbinger of death.

A BRIEF HISTORY OF RUM-RUNNING

By the 1800s the south coast of Newfoundland and the islands of Saint Pierre and Miquelon had established an intriguing precursor to what we might today call the Cultural Exchange. Settlers were driven from one region to the other in a series of treaties between the British and the French. Each region alternated from British to French rule, then back again, then switched again, and so on. The early residents of these areas were treated as pieces in an *Alice In Wonderland* chess game. The people of Saint Pierre were ordered to live on the south coast, the residents of the south coast were ordered to live on Saint Pierre, willy-nilly, until 1835.

In 1835 the House of Assembly of Newfoundland passed an act to "Prevent the encroachment of aliens on the fisheries of this Island." At that time, the fishermen of Saint Pierre and Miquelon were treating the waters of Newfoundland as their own personal scooping grounds for capelin and other bait. The new act put the stop to that activity (officially) but also prohibited Newfoundlanders from being able to sell bait to the French. (Which is what the fishermen of the south coast intended all along when they first complained about the overfishing by the French: to sell the capelin and other bait at a profit.)

That marked the beginning of the original smugglers' market. Newfoundland fishermen went to Saint Pierre on the sly to sell their capelin, mackerel, and other fish. While they were there, they thought it a wonderful thing to spend their profits on tea, sugar, tobacco, and rum! It was a fine give and take of under-the-counter enterprise. Consequently, the first sea patrols were launched and a long history of rum-running was on its sea legs.

An early draft of this play was produced by the Grand Bank Regional Theatre Festival. It has since been workshopped by the Resource Centre for the Arts, St. John's, and Theatre Newfoundland Labrador, and was produced by Theatre Newfoundland Labrador at the Gros Morne Theatre Festival from June 6 to September 20, 2008. It featured the following cast and creative team:

Jack: John Dartt
Frank: Colin Furlong
Jim: Evan White

Director: Jeff Pitcher
Stage manager: Karen Griffin
Set and prop design: Denyse Karn
Lighting design: Walter J. Snow
Costume design: Gaylene Buckle
Sound design: Sean Panting

CHARACTERS

Jim: A young fellow in his twenties. A newlywed and a dory builder who is afraid of the water. He is Frank's nephew.

Jack: Jack is in his sixties and is a bachelor who has seen and done it all.

Frank: Frank used to have his own schooner, but a tragedy caused him to lose everything. Unhappily married, he is in his forties.

Miss Tillie: A twenty-two-foot dory with an outboard motor, circa 1955.

Herself: The ocean.

TIME

Fall. Mid-1960s. Late at night.

PLACE

The open water between St. Pierre and Newfoundland.

LOCATION

The *Miss Tillie*.

ACT ONE

Darkness. We hear the distant sound of voices raised in anger and fright. Shouts ring out in French and English. We hear the sound of shots fired from a single rifle.

JACK: Run, b'ys, run!

FRANK: I'm running!

JIM: Wait for me!

JACK: Run faster!

JIM: I'm trying!

FRANK: I'm not waiting for you!

JIM: I'm running!

JACK: Run, ye sons of mothers! Run, ye dogs of heaven!

FRANK: Shut up, Jack!

We hear the shouts of the French pursuers.

JIM: What's he saying! What's he saying!

FRANK: He's saying run before he shoots the arse off you!

JIM: I can't see where I'm going!

JACK: Run, ye Christian mongrels!

JIM: Don't leave me!

FRANK: Come on!

JIM: Wait for me, b'ys!

FRANK: Run!

We hear the sound of splashing as the men run into the water and the thump of JIM rolling into the dory.

JIM: Ow, me head! Oh God oh God oh God. I'm here! I'm in! I'm in!

FRANK: Help us push off!

JIM is huddled in the bottom of the boat.

JIM: I'm in! I'm in! Let's go let's go let's go!

FRANK: Get out and help us push off!

JIM: I just got in, I'm not getting out!

We hear JACK and FRANK push the boat off.

FRANK & JACK: Heave!

FRANK: Jesus, she's heavy.

FRANK & JACK: Heave!

JIM: *(from inside the boat)* Put your backs into it!

JACK: Once more!

FRANK & JACK: Heave!

JIM: Hurry up hurry up hurry up!

We hear the groans of FRANK and JACK. We hear the sound of the boat being pushed off and we hear the splashes of JACK and FRANK jumping in the boat.

JACK: Start us up, Frank.

The French pursuers are closer. We hear their shouts. FRANK tries to start the dory motor. It catches and fails. Catches and fails again.

JIM: Oh frig oh frig / oh frig.

JACK: / Any time now, Frank old man. Start her up.

Lights slowly come up on the scene. Another shot rings out. FRANK tries to start the motor again. It catches and fails again.

FRANK: Oh fuck me.

JACK: Gentle with her, Frank.

JIM is unseen, still huddled in the bottom of the dory.

JIM: Hail Mary, full of grace, the Lord be with thee /

JACK: / Gentle but quick, / if you don't mind.

FRANK: / Jesus, Jack, it's a motor / not a two-dollar whore.

JIM: / Blessed art thou who forgives / us our trespasses among women—

JACK: / Now's a good time, Frank.

FRANK pulls again. The motor catches. They pull out. The sound of the motor continues throughout. The voices of the French pursuers are obscured and fade away. JACK takes off a battered fedora to wipe his brow and puts it back on.

Ah, *Miss Tillie*, that's me good girl.

JIM: / Now and at the hour of the fruit of our womb, Jesus, Mary, and Joseph R. Smallwood.

JACK: Amen to that.

Pause. The men catch their breath.

FRANK: I got to give up smoking.

Pause.

JIM slowly pokes his head up and clutches the side of the boat.

JIM: I never saw the likes of that before in my life! My heart is up in my throat. I'm sure I can feel it. Feel it, Jack. Can a person's heart get lodged in their throat?

JACK: If your heart doesn't choke you, I will. Keep it down!

JIM: I'm only saying!

FRANK: Jack.

JACK: What?

FRANK: Do me a favour.

JACK: What?

FRANK: Pick him up and throw him overboard.

JIM: I'm only saying.

FRANK: Why didn't you get out and help us?

JIM: I didn't want to get my head blown off.

FRANK: No, better for me and Jack to get blown away, is that it?

FRANK makes a grab for JIM but misses.

Ya coward.

JACK: Crowd of French jackals.

JIM: I thought we were dead.

JACK: Only if they caught us.

JIM: They were shooting at us!

JACK: They were shooting over our heads, you great eedgit.

JIM: Then how come you were running too?

JACK: Because that is how it's done, my son. They wave the gun and we run.

Pause. They look behind them.

JIM: Anyone coming?

FRANK: Not that I sees.

JIM: Will they chase us?

FRANK: Not that I knows.

JACK: Water's like the sheet of glass. We'll see land in no time.

FRANK: I'd rather have a bit of chop.

JIM: I'm glad there's no chop.

FRANK: *(to JACK, referring to JIM)* If that throws up again, I'll heave 'im out myself.

JIM: I gets seasick.

JACK: Stop your complaining. Both of ye.

FRANK: I told you he'd be dead weight.

JACK: And I told *you* me back is give out. I can't lift anything over ten pounds.

FRANK: Didn't slow you down none back there.

JACK: It only hurts when I bend over.

FRANK: Fool me once, Jack, fool me once.

JIM: *(to JACK)* How long more till we gets out of this?

JACK: How long more, Frank?

FRANK: Same as always.

JIM: Longer going back 'cause we're heavier.

FRANK: The usual amount of time.

JIM: But how long is that?

FRANK: What you'd expect.

JIM: Where's the compass?

FRANK: Don't need a compass.

JACK: We only need God's great compass.

FRANK: Jesus, Jack.

JACK: Stars and the moon above, and the heavenly currents of Herself beneath.

JIM: Where are we going to put in?

FRANK: Well, now. According to my bearings, if I plots our way from point A to point B. And then from point B to point C. Allows for the tide and the wind. Calculates from where I thinks we are, to where I thinks we wants to go, we should end up a couple of miles either way from where I thinks we should be.

JIM: Oh, God.

JACK: You never want to land in the same place twice anyhow.

JIM: I can't wait to kiss the dry land.

JACK: Jaysus. The last time a Frog pointed a gun at me was thirty years ago. Me and Vince Mitchell. You knew him, Frank.

FRANK: Lung disease.

JACK: Fluorspar mine.

FRANK: Fuckers.

JACK: Coughed his own lungs up. Anyway, me and him was on a run. We were loaded up, level to the gunnels we were. Vince had just paid off our supplier, old Marcelle, when from out of the darkness comes this young bruiser, François. Waving around a gun. Had two or three rowdies with him. Just like tonight.

JIM: I know you never got a fright.

JACK: Not right then. I got a start, first. Then I got a fright. This young François looks at me and Vince, and he says, *(with French accent)* "You always purchase your rum and cigarettes from Marcelle. But I think the time has come for you to give some of that money to me, if you want to get out of here alive!"

FRANK: I knows, now.

JACK: So Vince says, "Well, my son. What's this all about?" And François sneers at him, "I am not your son!" And Vince says, "Not that you knows of!"

FRANK: Had no lungs but he had balls on him.

JACK: Old Marcelle was just standing there with a big grin on his face. Nothing to him. He had his money in his pocket. Could have walked away and never looked back. But he looks at François and says, "O mon Dieu! You do not wish to come up on the wrong side of these fine gentlemen! Do you not know who they are?" And I says, "That's right!" And Vince says, "That's right! Don't you know who we are, b'y!" And then he says, "Who are we, again?" And Marcelle says, "They are close personal Newfoundland relations to the Capone family." "Oh, yes, that's right!" says Vince. "Good old Uncle Al!"

JIM: Al Capone?

JACK: Next thing we know, they're giving us armloads of bread and cheese and French wine. Telling us to give their best regards to Uncle Al Capone, and saying how they would never do anything ever again to cause us any grief. And Vince looks at the bread and cheese and says, "Got neither touton on ya, have ya?"

FRANK: (cynically) You're sure that's how it went, Jack?

JACK: I swear on a mountain of Gideon's Finest! They *says* Capone left his hat in the Hôtel Robért.

JIM: What was he doing in Saint Pierre?

FRANK: Teaching Sunday school, b'y.

JACK: Drinking with me on at least one occasion.

JIM: Now look what I'm after doing to meself. Got meself turned into a gangster. I suppose now I'll have some Chi-car-go mobster hunting me down and calling me "You dirty rat."

JACK: We're not gangsters.

JIM: Criminals, that's what we are.

JACK: Only technically.

JIM: According to the law.

JACK: The law only sets a man on a particular side of the universal fence.

JIM: What fence would that be?

FRANK: Jack's four-sided fence.

JACK: There's us on one side. The Mounties on one side. The Frogs on one side. And the gendarmes on one side. As long as everybody keeps to their own side of the fence, no one gets hurt.

JIM: Whoever heard tell of a four-sided fence. That doesn't add up.

JACK: Tradition has its own set of mathematics, Jim.

FRANK: Pass me the traditional flask.

JACK: Here.

JACK passes FRANK a flask. FRANK takes a very quick swallow and pockets the flask.

JIM: Why was that man firing a gun at us?

JACK: Not *at* us! Over our heads.

JIM: I guess he never heard tell of that four-sided fence with all the respect in it. Gave me such a fright I'll have to change me drawers when I get home out of it.

JACK: Don't talk to me about your old drawers. We've got to grease the wheel a bit more, that's all.

JIM: How's that?

JACK: The lookout man wants extra, I expect.

FRANK: We can't pay him any more, Jack. The more he gets the more he'll want.

JACK: Well, they were only giving us a warning tonight. Putting us on notice.

FRANK: Bit more than a warning, Jack.

FRANK holds up his sleeve. We see a large bullet hole in the fabric underneath his arm.

JIM: *(to JACK)* Thought you said they weren't really shooting at us.

JACK: Pass me the flask.

FRANK hands JACK the flask. JACK takes a quick swallow and puts the flask away. They check behind them. No one is following.

JIM: Stars have got the sky lit up like Grandmother's Christmas tree.

FRANK: It's too bright.

JACK: We are but a shadow in the night, Frank.

FRANK: Bit of chop makes you hard to spot.

JIM: We're too low in the water.

FRANK: We're all right, as long as those barrels don't roll around. You managed to get that done right, did you?

JIM: Yes, Uncle Frank. I've got them lashed up solid. Airtight. How much you think we'll get for them?

FRANK: Hard to say.

JIM: But how much do you think?

FRANK: The usual.

JIM: *(exasperated)* Jack?

JACK: We've got a decent haul.

FRANK: Plus the baccy. People will be parching for it after the big raid last month. Frigging Mounties.

JACK: They took Harold's truck. And his boat.

FRANK: They'll set fire to the truck and scuttle the boat in front of him. Bastards.

JACK: Left his missus on her own with two wee babes. I don't know what these modern times are coming to. It's getting so a man can't smuggle in peace. Too bad it was Harold had to go down.

JIM: Why did he have to go down?

FRANK: Never mind.

JACK: Keeps the Mounties off the rest of us for a while.

JIM: Why?

JACK: For the greater good. Now give it a rest, Jim, b'y.

JIM: He's in jail so we can be out here giving the Frenchies a bit of target practice. Next time I crosses water, it'll be on a bridge.

FRANK: *(to JIM)* What kind of a Newfoundlander are you? Hates to be on the water.

JIM: I'm a boat builder.

FRANK: The dory man who's afraid of the water.

JACK: Leave him alone, Frank.

Pause.

Let me just say, Jim my boy, we'll be set up for a good while on this load.

JIM: Good, 'cause this is my first and last time at this racket.

FRANK: Get yourself a new boat out of it, Jack, why don't you.

JACK: There's nothing wrong with *Miss Tillie*.

FRANK: She's as slow as a crate.

JIM: Me and Father built this boat for Jack. I learned on this one when I was ten years old. You weren't around, so don't talk about her.

JACK: Oh, I know there are faster boats.

FRANK: My new one, now. She's a beauty. Runs like a whippet. Floats along on the air.

JIM: The Yanks are inventing boats that never get wet.

JACK: A boat that floats on the air is a boat with no heart.

FRANK: Mine frigging flies, when she gets going.

JACK: That's not a boat. That's a plane.

JIM: Oh, Uncle Frank's got himself a thoroughbred, all right.

FRANK: Fibreglass.

JACK: I don't believe in fibre-blasted.

JIM: It goes against nature to neglect the wood. You know what he went and done, Jack. Goes and buys a speedboat off a "dealership" in St. John's.

JACK: Waste of good money.

FRANK: It's the sixties, not the frigging forties anymore. The Mounties have got the fastest boat in the province. You've got to be able to outrun them.

JACK: It's not about outrunning, Frank. It's about outmanoeuvring. It's about cat and mouse, my son. Cat and mouse. How's the cat and mouse supposed to play if all you're trying to do is win a race?

JIM: Just ask him where his boat is now.

JACK: Where?

FRANK: I've got her hid up the shore.

JIM: You sure she's not floatin' over the beach, like a frigging cloud?

FRANK: Jesus, b'y. The Mounties have been watching me like a hawk.

JACK: That's another thing I don't believe in. Mounties.

FRANK: They know I've got her, only they can't figure out where I've got her hid. I can't go get her. They got a plainclothes on me so tight if I bent over he could scratch me arse.

JACK: Oh, yes. The mainlander who's boarding over to Cochranes'.

JIM: Says he's out this way doing a *survey*. Hair down around his shoulders like he's Peter Francis Quinlan.

JACK: That's his idea of looking like a local.

FRANK: Well, I has a bit of fun with him. I goes down to the beach and I saunters along, nice and easy. Gives him a chance to catch up with me. I rolls up a smoke. He pulls out a *store-bought*. I stops to look at the water. He stops to look at the water. I bends over to have a look at something. He bends over to look at something. I darts up in the woods. He darts up in the woods. I has a leak. He's got no choice. He's got to whip it out and have a leak. I've got that boat hidden so good he's after stepping on her two or three times, if he only knew.

JIM: Fat lot of good to have a new-fangled boat and can't get at it.

FRANK: It's worth the satisfaction.

JIM: Me and Jack should've done this run ourselves. Left you home walking on the beach.

FRANK: I'm the one with the connections.

JIM: The connection who tried to shoot us.

FRANK: Turning up with you in tow set him on edge.

JIM: It wasn't me who set him on edge.

FRANK: *(to JACK)* I told you it wouldn't go over. Turning up with a stranger.

JIM: All you had to do was tell him I was your nephew. He would of relaxed.

FRANK: *You* relax.

JIM: No, *you* relax.

FRANK: You relax.

JIM: You relax. Once this trip's over you won't have to look at me for another ten years.

JACK: There's a saying I recall. "You're better off fighting with your own pack of savages than someone else's pack of savages."

JIM: There's another saying. If the devil comes at you with a smile on his face, watch out for his teeth, 'cause he's coming in for a shark attack. Or in Uncle Frank's case, watch out for his dentures, 'cause he's got neither tooth in his head.

FRANK: I've got my own teeth.

JIM: Have not.

FRANK: I bought 'em and paid for 'em.

JIM: That don't make them real.

JACK: News to me.

Pause.

FRANK: When I was a boy I got a toothache one time. Too much lassy on my bread. We could never afford sugar but we always had that old black lassy. So I gets this big old toothache and Mother hauls me off to see this missus in Fortune who could cure anything with her hot bread poultice. She had a magic spell she could put on you, if the moon was right. But she takes one look in my mouth and says, "My God! This young fella's teeth are black!" And Mother says, "I make no wonder his teeth are black, sure he never lays off the lassy!" So the missus gives me the big dose of rum and hauls out all my teeth with a pair of pliers. There was nothing magic about that. And Mother says, "My God, what did you haul out all his teeth for!" And the missus says, "To save you the next twenty trips down to see me."

JIM: Did you never hear tell of a toothbrush?

FRANK: A toothbrush is only for a man got nothing better to do than stand around and stare at his own mouth all day long.

Pause.

JIM: How much longer do you think, before we makes land? Lizzie will be wondering about me.

JACK: You never told her what we were up to.

JIM: No, my God, no. I knows better than that.

JACK: You sure, now? Ye being newlyweds and all.

JIM: I told her there was a fellow in Mooring Cove needed a few repairs on his skiff. She thinks I'm working on that for the better part of the night. But she'll be missing me. This is the first night we've been apart since we got married.

JACK: She's a sweet one, your Lizzie.

FRANK: Got a nice set on her.

JIM: Mind your mouth!

FRANK: Set of teeth! Teeth! Got all her own teeth.

JACK: Lovely smile on her. It's a wonder you can tear yourself away for a night.

JIM: We needs money for the baby.

FRANK: Ye got neither baby.

JIM: We will in seven months' time.

JACK: Congratulations, my son.

FRANK: Well, well. Who would have thought you had it in ya.

JIM: Shows what you knows. Lizzie says I got... never mind.

JACK: Says what?

JIM: Never mind.

FRANK: Look at his ears, turning all pink.

JIM: Lizzie says I've got a fine profile on me.

FRANK: A fine profile. What's that?

JACK: Well, b'y, I never heard a fellow's "manhood" called a profile before.

JIM: Jeez, b'y! It means I cuts a fine figure of a man, whenever I turn sideways.

FRANK: Yeah, till the honeymoon's over.

JIM: Lizzie always said she fell in love with my profile first.

JACK: Sounds like a word a schoolteacher would use.

FRANK: And what a sweet little schoolteacher like Lizzie sees in you, I'll never know.

JIM: Well, you've got me there. That's what I wonders about too. Me, who never wrote more than two words in my life till my wedding night.

JACK: How's that now?

JIM: I'm not telling. Ye'll laugh at me.

JACK: I won't laugh.

JIM: He will.

JACK: He won't.

FRANK: I'm not saying nothing.

JIM: Well, I'm good with calculations and measuring. But we all know I was never good on the books. Seeing as how I had to quit school when Father passed on.

JACK: Carry on.

JIM: I never told Lizzie. She was always reading poetry and stories, and when she'd try to get me to read to her I'd make out like my eyes were bad. Till our wedding day.

JACK: Now that was a scoff. And a fine scuff, too.

JIM: Well, when we get in to our little house, and just before we get ready to... you know.

JACK: Ready to... turn in for the night.

JIM: Right. Ready to turn in for the night. Well, Lizzie takes out this little Bible she was after saving up for. And she says, "This is going to be our family Bible from now on. We're going to write our names and all the important family dates in it." And she writes her name down, and then she passes me the pen.

JACK: You told her you couldn't see properly, right?

JIM: She hauls out this magnifying glass, so I can see where to put my name.

FRANK: I suppose you got an earful.

JIM: No. Shows how much you knows. I says to her, I says, "Lizzie. I know numbers, and I can tell how long a plank is just by sizing it up. But I don't know how to read or write." And she says, "A fine figure like yourself can't be expected to learn everything all at once. Your brain'd get stogged up." And we sat down right then and there and started on the ABCs.

Pause.

FRANK: When did you get around to the birds and the bees?

JACK: He got around to it. He's got a youngster on the way.

JIM: When my young fellow is born, I'll write his name into the Bible myself.

FRANK: How do you know it's a boy?

JIM: Lizzie got a sixth sense.

JACK: —Listen! Listen!

JIM: What's wrong?

JACK: Cut the motor, Frank. Cut the motor.

FRANK cuts the motor. They listen. They hear the motor of another craft off in the distance. It sounds heavy and modern, not like their own putt-putt.

Listen.

JIM: Oh no. Who is it? Who is it!

FRANK: She's got her running lights on. Biggish.

JACK: Ssssh. It's so bloody calm. Do you think she heard us?

FRANK: Not over the sound of her own engine.

JACK: Sound travels on a night like this.

FRANK: We've got no lights on, she can't see us.

JACK: Unless she's on the hunt. Turns on that big spotlight, then she'll have us.

FRANK: Take it easy now, men. Take it easy. We'll just stay as we are and let her mosey on by, nice and easy as you please.

JIM: Oh, please don't let us get caught. Please don't let us get caught. Please don't let us get caught—

JACK: Hold your tongue.

They listen and watch.

Jaysus. Yup. That's the Mountie cutter. I can tell by her *profile*.

JIM: We're sunk.

JACK: They're just out prowling around. Not looking for us in particular.

FRANK: They might as well have a church bell ringing, with all those lights on.

JACK: Nice looking cutter.

JIM: Built in Montreal. If they're going to be out on our water hunting us down, you'd think the least they could do is get a fine figure like me to build their boats for them.

JACK: She's all looks. Built too high for these waters. Look at the roll on her, and this a calm night. *Miss Tillie* won't be long getting the best of her.

JIM: I'm only saying. If I had any good business left these days, I wouldn't need to be out here at all hours with ye crowd.

FRANK: She's out of sight, but we'll keep the motor off for a few more minutes.

JACK: Now listen. There's a small cave out on the point, that's where we'll stash the barrels for the time being.

JIM: What about the baccy?

FRANK: There are ledges in the cave, the baccy will be fine. And the barrels will float.

JIM: Then what?

JACK: Then, nothing, Jim my son. Then, nothing. We carry on like butter wouldn't melt. Our friend with the truck will start moving it out over the road next week. We get our cut, and then we still lie low.

FRANK: Sit on that money like it's a cushion sewed to your backside. That's what gets a fellow caught. Spending up a storm, buying this and that, drinking like fools and bragging.

JACK: Lie low and put the poor mouth on ya, and we'll all make out fine.

JIM: Well, ye won't have to worry about me none. I'm not going around spending money.

FRANK: Good.

JIM: I'm only going to build a nice big back piece onto the house.

JACK: You can't build a back piece onto your house! Where will you say the money came from!

JIM: It's only lumber!

FRANK: Dim as the day is long.

JACK: Start us up again, Frank. I'd say we're after losing a good half hour now.

JIM: Frigging current.

FRANK: The current is vicious out here. Look at the sky. The stars are not where I'd like them to be. We've been drifting.

He tries to start the motor. It sputters and fails. He pulls at it again. It sputters and fails.

JIM: Jack? Where's the spare motor?

JACK: What spare motor?

JIM: The spare motor to pick up the slack if the main motor conks out.

JACK: Oh, I never use a spare motor.

FRANK: Where's the oars?

JACK: Oh, I got oars.

JIM: Good. Where are they?

JACK: Out behind the shed.

FRANK: Oh fuck me.

FRANK tries to start the motor again. It sputters and fails.

JIM: What are we supposed to do now?

JACK: Pray.

FRANK: Jesus.

JACK: You've got her flooded, that's all. Give it a minute.

FRANK: It doesn't sound flooded to me.

JACK: There's nothing wrong with that motor.

FRANK: Yeah. That's what Rick Drover used to say. Nothing wrong with his motor either. Till he went out on a run and ran out of gas.

JACK: Rick Drover is thick as a plank.

JIM: What happened to him?

FRANK: He was adrift for two days before the Mounties picked him up.

JACK: And him with a full load aboard.

FRANK: He was waving at the cops, telling them to come ahead, hold on, come ahead, hold on, while he was throwing it all overboard. He was drunk by that time, alone in a boat for two days with nothing but a load of rum to talk to.

JACK: The rum and baccy rolled ashore for a week after that. Rolled ashore like the capelin. They were fishing up rum and baccy everywhere.

JIM: Oh Lordy. We're sunk.

JACK: We're not sunk. We're drifting.

JIM: I can't swim.

JACK: No point in knowing how to swim anyway. You'd get the hyper-hernia on a night like this.

JIM: Hypothermia, Jack.

JACK: Herself grabs hold of you and rocks you to sleep.

JIM: Well, as long as I only went to sleep. I wouldn't want to drown.

JACK: Don't go swimming in the first place and you won't go drowning, that's my motto.

JIM: But if you can't swim, you're going to drown.

JACK: So. Don't swim.

FRANK: No one is going drowning tonight.

JACK tries the motor again. It sputters and fails. He tries again. It catches and starts.

Pause.

JIM is visibly relieved. JACK looks smug. FRANK is irritated.

JACK: Anyway. Wait a good few months before you build that back piece onto your house. Make out like you hates to be at it, only for the wife is at you all the time. On account of the wee babe coming and all.

JIM: But Lizzie doesn't nag me about stuff like that.

JACK: No, but make out like she do.

JIM: Don't you want to do something nice for your wife, Uncle Frank? I hear she's a nice lady.

FRANK: My wife is hateful.

JACK: That's a shocking thing to say.

FRANK: Oh, no. She hates me.

JIM: That's awful.

JACK: That's life, Jim. That's life.

JIM: I couldn't live if Lizzie hated me.

JACK: Hate keeps people together better than love.

FRANK: Like you'd know.

JIM: What did you marry her for, if she's hateful?

FRANK: Change the subject, Jim.

JACK: She wasn't always hateful. Just like once upon a time he had teeth in his head.

JIM: Nothing will ever come between Lizzie and me.

JACK: Amen to that, Jim.

FRANK: Will ye two give it a fucking rest?

Pause.

JACK: Stars are gone.

FRANK: Bit of fog moving in.

JACK: I'm gut founded. Anyone want a capelin sandwich? The salty tidbits of the sea.

FRANK: Jesus, Jack, the heads are still on 'em.

JACK: The heads are where all the flavour is.

FRANK: I've got a few hard-time buns.

JIM: What's a hard-time bun?

FRANK: A raisin bun without the raisins.

JIM: Lizzie always makes sure we've got at least one raisin in every bun.

FRANK: And her with a bun in the oven.

JACK: Fog is coming up fast, Frank.

FRANK: We're all right. I wouldn't mind a good stiff breeze all the same.

JACK: Or a good stiff drink.

FRANK: Pass me the shine.

JACK passes FRANK the flask. They both take a quick sip. It's not the smoothest swalley in the world. The fog is moving in fairly quickly.

That's like the paint thinner. And us with the finest Saint Pierre rum on board.

JACK: Can't be at the merchandise.

JIM has pulled out a smoke and a pack of matches. He lights up a match.

JIM: Anyone want a smoke? I've got some rollies.

JACK smacks the match out of his hand.

JACK: You great wooden eedgit! Lighting up a match! Why don't you just set yourself on fire and jump up and down. See how long it takes that Mountie cutter to come breathing down our necks.

FRANK: Stunned as my hole. Stunneder.

JIM: There's no such word as stunneder.

JACK: How about arsehole! Is that a good enough word for you?

JIM: All right, all right!

Pause. JACK takes a bite out of a bun.

JACK: Good buns. Did your witch of a wife make 'em?

JIM: Won't she be worried about you?

FRANK: She thinks I'm gone to a Time down in Rushoon.

JIM: Without her?

FRANK: Oh, I invited her. I said, "Come on, Missus. Let's you and me go have a few laughs."

JIM: What would you have done if she'd said yes?

FRANK: I knew she wasn't going to say yes. If I say one thing, she wants to do another. As soon as I said I wanted to go to the Time in Rushoon, she wanted to traipse over to Fortune to visit her family. Had her very heart set on it all week, she said. "Well, why didn't you say so before this?" I asks her. " 'Cause you're supposed to *know* stuff like that," she says. So now she's gone off to Fortune in a huff, and as far as she knows I'm down to Rushoon, getting loaded, and carrying on with women half my age.

JACK: Ye crowd don't know how to run a marriage.

JIM: Look who's talking. No one wanted the likes of you.

JACK: Oh, lots wanted me.

JIM: Name one.

Pause.

Told you.

FRANK: Frigging fog. Shut your gobs and see if we can hear the foghorn.

JACK: Turn the motor off.

FRANK: That's what I won't. Listen, now.

Slow five count. They hear a distant foghorn. It continues throughout. FRANK *changes direction.*

Well, gentlemen. We are almost free and clear. And right under the noses of the frigging law.

JIM: Thanks be to God.

FRANK: What are you going to do with your share, Jack?

JACK: Well, after a few months' time, I'm boarding up the old house and I'm going in to St. John's. I'm getting a brand-new pair of dentures, the good kind.

JIM: What kind is that?

JACK: The kind that fits my mouth. Then, I'm going to Water Street and getting a brand-new suit at Wilansky's Haberdasheries. And that will be the first new suit I've had since I was six years old and made my first communion.

FRANK: Are you planning on dying or something?

JIM: What are you going to do with a new suit?

JACK: I'm going to get myself a nice room in a respectable boarding house in Brazil Square. I'm going to go to the card games at the B.I.S. every Saturday night, to the basilica for Mass every Sunday, and to the bingo every Monday. And I'm doing that until I get myself a good little woman.

FRANK: You don't need to be at all that. Just go buy yourself a woman for a night.

JACK: I don't want *that* kind of woman.

JIM: You're pulling my leg.

JACK: Ye laugh, now. I'm getting myself a good little woman, and I'm getting married. I've got a nice little bank account sove up. And the windfall from this run will be the icing on the cake. Or, the ring on the finger, so to speak.

FRANK: What kind of woman are you looking for? You can have mine.

JACK: I don't want a hateful woman. I don't want a sweet one either. I want a woman who is in between. One who doesn't expect too much, and one who is easy to get along with. Much like myself.

JIM: I thought you were never getting married.

JACK: I never said I was never getting married. I said ye crowd didn't know anything about it. It's taken me this long to figure out what makes a good marriage.

JIM: And what's that now?

JACK: Well. The man and the woman have each got to be content with their own company. So neither one is expecting the other one to do anything for them.

JIM: Sounds lonely to me.

FRANK: Sounds like heaven to me.

JACK: The beauty of it all is, if no one is expecting anything, then every time you do something, it's a wonderful thing! You've got to be companions. Then you can spend all your time playing cards, and having a mug up, or spinning a yarn in front of the fire.

JIM: If that's all I wanted I could live with you or Uncle Frank.

FRANK: I'd rather live with you than the wife.

JACK: I'll take her on a nice wedding trip. Probably take her over to the Hôtel Robért. Quit this smuggling racket and make a lawful trip to Saint Pierre for the first time in my life.

JIM: Good for you, Jack.

FRANK *gives* JACK *a skeptical look.*

JACK: Every time out I say to myself, "Jack, old man. You're getting too old for this. This is the last run." But then I think: one more time. One last time. I've been saying that for thirty years. But. The time has come.

JACK *lowers his voice.*

I'm letting Herself go and getting myself a warm-blooded woman in my bed.

JIM: Who's this "herself"? *Miss Tillie?*

JACK: No. Herself. *(whispers)* Herself.

FRANK *indicates the open water.*

FRANK: Her.

JIM: The water?

JACK: Keep your voice down.

JIM: Why?

JACK: She'll hear you.

Pause.

JIM: What are you going to do with your cut, Uncle Frank?

FRANK: I'm giving it all to the wife.

JIM: What?

JACK: I thought you said the wife was hateful.

FRANK: Oh, she is.

JIM: I'm sure she's not.

JACK: Don't you know your Aunt Roxie, Jim?

JIM: You knows I don't. So, what are you giving her all your money for?

FRANK: So she can set herself up in fine style. We got no youngsters. I'm giving her the money, and she can get herself one of those new-fangled phones she's always harping on about.

JACK: I miss the party-line phones.

FRANK: She wants one of those new phones now, what goes with the decor. Pink or peach or something. They're called a *rotary* phone.

JIM: A rotary phone?

FRANK: It's got a dial on it.

JACK: I took the phone out of the house. They puts the phone tap on, you now.

FRANK: Yes, Jim. You be careful what you talk about on the phone.

JIM: I wouldn't say anything.

JACK: They were listening in to Howard Clark there last spring. He was yakking it up with his girlfriend in Rushoon. He told her he was going on a run, and would she like some rum when he got back. Called his wife a weasel and said he'd like to set a snare for her. Went on and on about how he wouldn't sleep with the wife 'cause she put him in mind of the old hag. Well, the cops arrested him. And played the phone conversation at his trial. And the wife was sitting up in court, listening to the tape of him talking to the girlfriend.

FRANK: Well, the wife can yak to who she likes, once I'm gone. She can get herself all the mail-order dresses she likes out of the catalogue. She can charge whatever she wants over to Tibbo's Store. She can have a bag of raisins in every bun and a bag of sugar in every cup of tea, and a keg of lassy out by the door to wipe her feet in, if she wants.

JACK: But, what will you have left over for yourself?

FRANK: Freedom, Jack, my son. Freedom.

JIM: That's hard talk, Uncle Frank.

FRANK: Thought she caught a big fish when she caught me.

JACK: It's not your fault what happened.

FRANK: If I'd gone down with the boat she'd have more respect for me. I was the skipper.

JACK: No one blames you, Frank.

FRANK: Just another rum-runner. That's what she ended up with.

Pause.

JIM: I know a fellow from Point May. He hated his missus, too. So he left her and took up with her sister. Has your missus got a sister?

JACK: Jim. How did a boy like you ever end up with the lady school-teacher?

JIM: Well, you see, she's often remarked that she was as surprised as any-one to realize the depth of my personality.

JACK: Love is blind.

JIM: If she knew I was out at this tonight. Well. She got a temper.

FRANK: Don't start out asking permission for everything you do. Or you'll hate that new piece you builds on to your house.

JACK: Listen. Listen!

FRANK: Is it the Mountie?

JACK: No. Listen.

They hear whales in the distance.

JIM: Is it ghosts?

FRANK: Whales. Look at 'em. Look at 'em.

JACK: They're following us.

JIM: They're not too close, are they?

FRANK: Whales this time of year?

JACK: I saw four whales come right up out of the water one time, like rockets, all of them breaching at the same time. Up they came, weightless, the gorgeous big flukes on them.

JIM: What do they want?

FRANK: Just having a look.

They listen to the eerie sound of the whales breaching, blowing, singing. The fog is getting thick.

JIM starts to sing to the whales, very, very loudly.

JIM: "He took the whale right by the tail and turned it inside out! Oh! Jack was every inch a sailor." /

FRANK: / Shut your trap! You'll have the Mountie on us.

JIM: Only I like that part where he gets swallowed by the whale.

JACK: Like Jonah.

FRANK: Like who?

JACK: You great ignorant heathen.

FRANK: Who the frig is Jonah?

JIM: Jonah was a young fellow from up the shore. Won the lottery and went on a cruise one time.

FRANK: So?

JIM: So, what happened was, the ship got caught in a gale. And the passengers were shitbaked. Thought they were goners for sure. Everyone went right off the head. Went nuts. Went sea crazy.

FRANK: Jonah who?

JIM: It was in all the papers. This crowd was a right pack of savages. They threw Jonah over the side of the boat. Like a sacrifice, to get the storm to stop. Then, this whale rose up, right from out of the water, and swallowed Jonah before he had time to cross hisself.

FRANK: Poor fucker.

JIM: No, b'y. That whale kept Jonah inside him for three days and three nights. Talk about your heartburn. Next thing you know, that whale carries Jonah to shore and spits him out. Jonah had an excellent life after that. Built himself a house in Lamaline.

Beat. Four count. The whales are close now.

FRANK: Do you want my other leg? Or did you just want to pull the one.

JIM: Who's to say it's not true?

FRANK: I knows, now.

JACK: It's a Bible story, b'y.

JIM: Lizzie read it to me one time. Good one, hey?

A plume of spray interrupts them.

JACK: Jaysus, they're close. Look look look!

JIM: What's he doing!

JACK: Gone underneath the boat.

The men follow the whale as it dives beneath and surfaces on the other side.

FRANK: What's he at?

JACK: Jaysus, there he goes.

JIM: There's another one cutting in front of us, Uncle Frank.

FRANK: I sees him. I got the right of way. He can go fish.

JACK throws something overboard.

JIM: What's that?

JACK: Capelin sandwiches. Thought they might like a snack.

The whales retreat slightly. The men watch and listen.

I saw a mermaid once.

JIM: You never, Jack.

JACK: I was out squid-jigging. It got foggy and quiet, like it is now. I could feel something pulling on the rope, pulling hard. I thought I must have snagged a small shark. And up she came, my son.

JIM: You're the one who's codding now.

JACK: She rose up out of the water and looked me straight in the eye. She had long brown hair, all wet and plastered against her skull. It had conches living in it. She had big green eyes with no eyelids. And gills on her neck, sucking in and out. Half woman and half fish, she was. She had hold of my line and she pulled on it like a savage, like she was trying to haul me overboard. I think she was mad at me for jigging the squid. She pulled the line out of my hands and swam away, her and the squid behind her. I never went squid-jigging again.

JIM: How come?

JACK: She had no lips on her face, and two rows of teeth in her mouth like jagged saws. I wouldn't want her coming back for me a second time.

JIM: I hates the frigging water.

Pause. Ten count. The whale sounds recede yet again.

FRANK: I've got a better story than that.

JACK: I doubt it.

FRANK: I seen a fetch out on the water one time.

JIM: Now you got me creeped right out.

FRANK: The day my boat went down. Grandmother appeared before me, just standing on the water, if you don't mind.

JIM: What was she wearing?

FRANK: Wearing her housecoat and slippers.

JIM: Think she would have put on her raincoat, if she was going out on the water.

FRANK: I'm clinging on to the side of the boat, me and my crew. And I look up and there's Grandmother, just as plain as you please. And she says to me, "Well, my son, you'll make it this time. It was nice knowing you." And then she disappeared.

JIM: No.

FRANK: After we got picked up and made it back to shore, I found out that was the very minute she passed away. She had a heart attack while she was taking a nap. Went in her sleep.

JACK: Listen.

JIM: Stop trying to give me the willies.

JACK: I mean it. Listen!

FRANK: I don't hear anything, Jack, b'y.

JIM: Is it the whales?

FRANK: The whales are gone. Something spooked 'em.

JIM: You spooked them, with your old fetch.

JACK: Oh my good God, Frank. Cut her! Cut her!

FRANK: What?

JACK: *(pointing into the blackness)* Look! Coming for us!

FRANK: Jesus.

JIM: What is it? Is it a whale?

JACK: Hold on, Jim. Cut her, Frank!

FRANK: She's coming too fast!

We hear the sound of a heavy engine and see the huge shadow of a large vessel bear down on Miss Tillie.

We're too heavy, we're not going to make it!

JACK: We'll make it! Cut her!

JIM: Oh, Lordy. It's a boat! It's a boat! She's got no lights!

FRANK: Neither do we!

JACK: She don't see us! She don't see us!

Blackout. We hear the splintering sound of Miss Tillie *being torn asunder by the larger craft. We hear the sound of the mystery ship moving out of earshot, then only the lopping of the water.*

End Act One.

Intermission.

ACT TWO

In the darkness we hear waves, the ocean. We hear JIM screaming.

JIM: Uncle Frank! Uncle Frank!

Lights up. The fog is still thick but we can see what remains of Miss Tillie. Her prow is intact, canted upward at an unnatural angle. The barrels of rum float around and behind her, lashed to the places where she's broken. Debris floats around her.

Uncle Frank! Hold on!

We see JIM back on, half out of the boat, straining to haul FRANK up out of the water.

Hold on! Hold on to me!

The weight of FRANK almost hauls JIM down into the water.

I can't hold you! Uncle Frank, I can't hold you! You're hauling me under!

FRANK: Don't let go!

JIM: Help me!

FRANK: Don't let go, you son of a bitch!

JIM: Okay okay okay. I got you. I got you.

He pulls with all his might, pulling what he thinks is FRANK into what's left of the boat, but ends up clutching FRANK's oilskin.

(at the top of his lungs) Uncle Frank!!! You shagger!!!

FRANK: *(weakly)* Here.

JIM: I can't reach you!

FRANK: Jesus, Jim. Help me. *(weaker still)* Here.

JIM hunkers down in the wreckage.

JIM: I'll fall in I'll fall in I'll fall in I'll fall in. Oh, Lizzie Lizzie Lizzie. Help me, Lizzie.

FRANK: *(third time weakest)* Here.

JIM reaches into the water and just manages to grab FRANK by one arm. The weight of FRANK hauls JIM out of the boat, but his foot hooks on a piece of rope. JIM dangles headfirst into the water. FRANK gets his arm over the boat and, using JIM's prone body, manages to haul himself in.

I got to quit smoking.

He grabs JIM by the backside and pulls with all his might, screaming.

Aaaaagggggghhhhhh!

JIM slithers over the side like a giant fish, almost capsizing what's left of Miss Tillie. *They both lie there, shaking, dragging the air into them. JIM spits out water.*

JIM: Oh God oh God oh God oh God.

FRANK looks around at what they are floating in.

FRANK: Lord Jesus. Where's Jack?

JIM: Gone gone gone gone.

FRANK: Jack! Jack!

JIM: She tore right through us.

FRANK: Jack! Jack!

JIM: Flicked us around like a daisy.

FRANK: Jack! Shut up, Jim. Listen! Listen!

They hear JACK's voice from off in the distance. Each time he speaks his voice comes from a different direction, and from farther and farther away.

JACK: Help! Help me!

JIM: Jack!

JACK: Boys! Boys! Where are ye?

FRANK: Jack, b'y, we're in the boat.

JACK: Boys! Jim! Help me, for the love of God!

JIM: I can't see him.

FRANK: Are you able to make a swim for it?

JACK: I'm floating on top of something. But I'm getting waterlogged!

FRANK: Jack! Kick off your boots! And take off your sweater!

JACK: I'm not taking off my sweater!

FRANK: You've got to stay light! Take off your frigging sweater!

JACK: Not my fisherman's knit! Nan made it for me before she had her stroke!

FRANK: Take it off!

JACK: How will they know it's me if I die without my fisherman's knit on?

FRANK: Take off that sweater!

Pause. Slow count to six. FRANK *and* JIM *search the murky night in vain for a glimpse of* JACK.

Jack?

JACK: I've got it off. But, if Nan was alive, she'd kill me now.

FRANK: Can you kick your way over?

JACK: Oh. I'm losing my breath.

FRANK: Save your strength! We'll see if we can get to you.

(to JIM*)* Have we got anything to paddle with?

JIM *laughs in desperation.*

Jack? Hold on for a spell till I figures out what to do.

JACK: *(faintly)* Any time now would be good, lads.

JIM: What hit us, Uncle Frank? What hit us, what hit us, what hit us!

FRANK: Shut up now, Jim. We've got to get to Jack.

JIM: We've got no oars, b'y.

FRANK: That old fucker.

JIM: We're goners, Uncle Frank.

FRANK: Get a grip, b'y, get a grip.

JIM: What hit us?

FRANK *looks at the destruction of the boat, at the debris which surrounds them.*

FRANK: I don't rightly fucking know at the moment, Jim. Jesus Jesus Jesus.

JIM: No running lights, see. No running lights on her or us, see. Bad bad bad bad.

JACK: Help! Help me!

FRANK: Jack! Jack! We're here!

JACK: Here, I'm over here!

FRANK: You got to make a swim for it, Jack!

JACK: Me boots are full of water. I can't kick them off. I'm only afloat here on a few boards!

FRANK: Paddle toward the sound of my voice.

JACK: I can't tell where ye are.

FRANK: *(to JIM)* Have we got anything to shine?

JIM: There's water coming in, Uncle Frank. Make it stop. Make it stop, will you?

FRANK: Name of God, Jim, you got to help me out here.

JIM: That's too much water, Uncle Frank. Make it stop.

JACK: *(farther away this time)* Boys, can ye hear me? Boys?

FRANK: Current is pulling him out.

JACK: *(barely audible)* Herself has got me.

JIM: Our Father, who art in heaven. Hallowed be thy name. Thy king-dom come, thine will be done— /

FRANK: / Stop that.

JIM: / What's the next part? I always forgets the next part. Our Father who art in heaven. Hallowed be thy name. Thy kingdom come, thine will be done. /

FRANK: / Stop it.

JIM: / On earth.

FRANK: / Stop it.

JIM: / As it is in heaven.

FRANK: / Stop it.

Pause.

Here's Jack's tin cup. Bail with this.

JIM: Might as well use a thimble.

JIM starts to bail and rarely stops for the duration.

FRANK: Use your hands for all I care. Use something. Look. There's rope. Give me that. I'll plug 'er up. Now use the eyes in your head and look around. You're the boat builder and this is the fucking boat. Tell me what the fuck is going on.

JIM: Built my own coffin when I helped build this.

FRANK strips off his soaking sweater and pulls on his oilskin. JIM takes off his own oilskin, hauls off his own sweater, leaving on his flannel shirt. He gives the sweater to FRANK.

FRANK: Jim. This is as wet as mine was.

JIM: Cinch the cracks with it.

JIM calms down a bit as he surveys the damage.

Whatever hit us sliced us like bread. The force of it was so strong… it almost… the barrels all popped up, they're wedged in the breach. I think. They're lashed together pretty good.

FRANK: What's keeping us afloat?

JIM: The rum barrels. They're airtight. We'd better not shift our weight around any.

FRANK: What have we got left? Rope.

JIM: Motor's gone.

JIM laughs again.

The whole flipping stern is gone. Got a few planks here. We could try to paddle but I don't know what will happen if we start moving around.

FRANK: A couple of planks. Good. That's good.

JIM: Don't try to make out like we're going to be all right.

FRANK reaches over and smacks JIM in the face. Silence.

FRANK: Jack! Jack…!

No reply.

Well. Jack is smart. He won't be losing his head.

JIM: The water is too cold.

FRANK: As long as his heart is up out of it, up floating on something, he'll be all right. It's when your heart and lungs are down in the water that the hyper-hernia sets in.

JIM: My rollies are dry, but the matches are wet. How about that.

FRANK: When I bought the new speedboat, the fellow who sold her to me said he'd throw in a couple of life jackets, for free. I laughed at him.

JIM: Not that Jack would have life jackets on board. Look. Capelin sandwiches.

FRANK: The old fart.

JIM: JACK! JACK! Where are you?!

FRANK: Jack! Jack!

Long pause. No reply. FRANK and JIM look at each other.

JACK! JACK! JACK! JACK! YOU OLD FUCKER! ANSWER ME! JACK!

He screams himself hoarse.

JIM: He's gone, Uncle Frank.

FRANK: You shut up.

JIM: *You* shut up.

FRANK: Don't you give up on him!

JIM: No one knows where we are.

FRANK: You think I don't feel bad enough?

JIM: I'm only saying!

FRANK: That Mountie is out here somewhere.

JIM: I'll take jail over this, any day of the week.

FRANK: Would you now?

JIM: Wouldn't you?

Pause.

I said it would be my first and last time. I just didn't think my last time alive.

FRANK: Don't, Jim.

JIM: I wonder which side of the fence this puts us on.

FRANK: How do you mean?

JIM: That four-sided fence Jack was talking about. I wonder which side of the fence allows for this type of event.

FRANK: Must be a five-sided fence.

JIM: I broke me promise. Serves me right.

FRANK: What promise?

JIM: Father.

FRANK: What about him?

JIM: He told me a story one time.

FRANK: So?

JIM: He said the spirits of drowned fishermen live on the bottom of the ocean. They walk around down there waiting.

FRANK: Waiting for what?

JIM: Waiting to see a pair of legs they can grab onto and haul down. They're lonely down there. They think if they can catch hold of a living person that they'll bring life back into their bones. It never works but they keeps trying. "Next time," they thinks. "Next time." They're waiting to find the one person who can bring them back to life.

Beat.

Father said it was me.

FRANK: What was "you"?

JIM: He said I'm the one person that the dead are waiting for.

FRANK: Jesus, Jim. Your old man. What a piece of work.

JIM: He made me promise never to go out on the water. He told me this would happen.

FRANK: He was messin' with your head.

JIM: Poor old Jack will be down there walking around now.

FRANK: Dead men don't walk. And Jack's all right. He's out of earshot, that's all. Shut up about it, I told you, or I'll…

JIM: You'll what?

FRANK: Nothing.

JIM: Or what? You'll throw me overboard? Go ahead. It's what you wants to do.

FRANK: Leave it.

JIM: Dead weight, right, Uncle Frank? Like Mother and me and the rest of us after Father passed on?

FRANK: I knew when Jack turned up with you this was no good. Said you had him pestered to death.

JIM: He came to me! He knew I was on hard times. He knew I got a family to support. Not that you'd know anything about sticking by your family.

FRANK: You don't know nothing.

JIM: I knows this is my last chance to pound you.

He begins to pummel FRANK. FRANK *holds him off.* JIM *nearly topples over-board, losing his balance for a split second.* FRANK *grabs him by the arm just in time.*

(screaming) WHAT HIT US? WHAT HIT US? WHAT THE FUCK HIT US?

FRANK: Jim. Jim. Jim. She had no running lights on. Someone up to no good.

JIM: Like us. Like us. Like me.

FRANK: Could have been foreign. There are boats in these waters that we don't know the half of. Could have been a tanker. Dumping off something illegal.

JIM: Could have been a ghost ship.

FRANK: Could have been a giant squid, Jim. It makes no difference now.

JIM: I seen a giant squid one time. Sixteen footer washed up on the beach.

FRANK: Jack's mermaid.

Pause.

JIM: I thought it would be quick cash. For the baby.

FRANK: Well, this'll be a fine tale to tell that youngster when he's born.

JIM: Lizzie. She got a sixth sense. She'll know I was up to no good.

FRANK: How did the likes of you end up with her?

JIM: She came out from Corner Brook to go teaching. Took the train to Goobies. Took her five days to get all the way out to Grand Bank, on Foote's Taxi. We were after having that much rain; they were all stuck on the other side of a wash out, down over the road. I thought, that school-marm must have some gumption on her. I thought she was going to be an old spinster.

FRANK: Is this going to be a long story?

JIM: They asked me to redo the roof of the schoolhouse for her, and get the place all spic and span. Only for we had a spell of rain. It rained for twenty-six and a half days straight. So, the rain finally clears off. I climbs up on the roof of the schoolhouse, thinking, I've got tons of time. And then I see this missus traipsing through the muck with a satchel, and books, and a fine-looking hat on her head. I pops up out of a hole in the roof and says, "How do you do, Missus!" And I gave her such a start she screamed and fell over in the muck. And she gave *me* such a start, I fell off the roof. And the both of us ended up in the hospital with sprained ankles. Then I saw she wasn't a missus at all. She was a miss.

FRANK: And she seen you were a great big eedgit.

They bail for a while, JIM *with the cup,* FRANK *with his bare hands. Both men are shaking badly. They hear the whales off in the distance. They listen.*

JIM: Oh no.

JIM *almost cries.*

I'm sorry. I'm sorry.

FRANK: What's wrong with you?

JIM: Me fingers is froze and the cup just slid right out of me hand. I lost the tin cup. We got nothing to bail with.

FRANK: We're all right. Come here.

JIM: What for?

FRANK: So I can get me arms around you.

JIM: Bit late for a family hug.

FRANK: We got to get our body heat up, b'y.

FRANK gets his arms around JIM.

JIM: When me and Lizzie were courting we used to go out for hot fudge sundaes. I'd love a hot fudge sundae.

FRANK: People don't court anymore. They go out on *dates*.

JIM: A date means what day of the year it is. That just doesn't give a woman the importance she deserves.

FRANK: You've got the soul of an old-timer, Jim. I'd say it's your handiwork kept this one from splintering up like toothpicks.

JIM: We'd be dead already if we were in your fibreglass contraption.

FRANK: I daresay.

JIM: Might be better off if we were.

FRANK: So that's what she meant by "this time."

JIM: Who?

FRANK: Grandmother. When her fetch came to see me, when my boat went down. She said, "You'll make it back *this* time." Like she knew there was going to be another time.

JIM: What was it like, when you lost the boat?

FRANK: One minute we were standing on deck. "What the fuck is *that?*" one fellow said to me. Next thing I know, the boat is on her side and the lot of us are clinging on, gulping down the briny water, gasping for air. We were holding on to each other, holding on to the boat, and her slowly sinking.

JIM begins to stir, begins to rummage around. He lashes two boards together in the shape of a cross.

JIM: If I put my oilskin over this, I don't know. I might be able to rig up some kind of sail.

FRANK: It was a rogue wave got us. Came out of nowhere. It blacked out the sky, had us on our side and fighting for our lives in less than thirty seconds.

JIM: You saved all your men.

FRANK: Trawler out of Harbour Breton saw us go over. That's the only thing that saved us, because we sure never had time to get a mayday out.

JIM props up a makeshift sail.

It looks like a cross.

JIM: Might catch a bit of wind. Look. What's that?

FRANK: What?

JIM: In the water.

JIM fishes something out of the water and hauls it in.

FRANK: It's Jack's sweater.

FRANK begins to weep, big bawling sobs coming out of him.

JIM: *(begins to sing)* "Rock of ages, cleft for me;
Let me hide myself in thee,
Let the water and the blood."

JIM continues to sing and hum throughout FRANK's confession, seemingly oblivious to what FRANK is telling him.

FRANK: I come inshore with a load one night. The calmest kind of night. Not a star in the sky, it was black as tar. You could hold your arm straight out and not see your own hand. Me and the boys unloaded, and then, by the fuck. Didn't we hear this roar from up the beach. "Stay where you are, gentlemen. Hands up in the air." Someone was after rattin' us out.

JIM: *(singing)* "From thy wounded side which flowed,
Be of sin the double cure;
Save from wrath and make me pure."

FRANK: The boys took off in the dark, tripping up over each other, and cursing and swearing. They weren't long getting the cuffs slapped on. But see, I figured the best thing to do was lie low and hide in plain sight. Just keep still until the racket died down. So I just lay down on the beach in the dark, just like that. If they didn't shine a light directly on me there was no way they were going to see me.

JIM continues to hum.

This Mountie comes crunching along on the beach. Walked right by me two or three times. Took his time. Took about an hour he did, with me there underneath his feet the whole time, holding my breath. He was that close to me, I could've reached up and brushed his teeth for him. Anyway. He turned around to leave, and I only went and let out the big frigging sneeze. "Bless you," he says. "Thanks," I says. "You're under arrest," he says. "No problem," I says. And that was that. Nice feller. Bought me a feed of fish and chips on the way to the cop shop.

JIM continues to hum.

We all got caught, see. But only one went down for the greater good.

A giant plume of water shoots up beside them. A whale. They hear the whales spouting and singing.

Jack sent a heavenly chorus.

JIM: Uncle Frank, your hands are blue.

JIM lifts FRANK's hands to his mouth, blowing on them.

FRANK: Jesus, Jim, I'm only having a rest for a minute.

JIM: Frig off with your "rest."

The makeshift sail slowly tips over to one side and with a splash slides into the water, leaving them with nothing.

FRANK: Sorry I got you into this, Jim.

JIM: I wanted to.

FRANK: I should have told you to stay home and whittle.

JIM: When Father got sick. You took off to the States to find yourself. Father said you went to California to work at Disneyland. Said you were having an affair with Snow White.

FRANK: Five-year stretch in Dorchester.

JIM: Hope you found yourself.

FRANK: I swore. Swore to your father I'd stay clear of you and keep you away from it. Swore on a stack of Bibles.

JIM: Gideon's Finest.

FRANK: He said he wouldn't tell you I was in jail as long as I kept clear. Some get themselves locked up and they turn into crybabies, trying to make deals. Some go in, they keep their head down, and they cross the days off the calendar, one by one. They watch the time go by, and they don't complain. My first time in, two or three of the guards was after buying all their Christmas rum off me. I never said anything. They never said anything. I wasn't going to sing any tunes.

Pause.

All I got out of it was a few thousand dollars and a wife who saw me for the big fat sucker I am.

JIM: We'll both go down for the greater good now.

FRANK: Fuck.

JIM: If it keeps my own youngster off the water... I'm sending my fetch to see Lizzie. I'm trying to heave it out of me. Do you see it? Any sign of it?

FRANK: I'll send *my* fetch to see Lizzie. You can send *your* fetch to see my wife. Tell her I said not to expect any letters.

JIM: Nope. I'll be sending my fetch to Lizzie. I'll tell her I loves her half to death. I loves her all to pieces. I loves her half in two. I love the way she fills our little house with nice warm things that smell good.

FRANK: My wife fills the house with nagging.

Beat.

She fills the house with silence.

JIM: She can't be that bad, Uncle Frank.

FRANK: Jack is... Jack was right. It isn't her. It's the both of us together.

JIM: If you could send your fetch to see her, what would you tell her?

FRANK: Frig off.

JIM: What have you got to lose, Uncle Frank?

Beat.

FRANK: I'd tell her it isn't her who's hateful. It's me.

JIM: That sounds about right.

They listen to the whales. Both men are half gone.

Uncle Frank.

FRANK: Eh?

JIM: Throw me overboard.

FRANK: What?

JIM: I can't stand the thought of sinking slowly like this. Throw me overboard so I can get it over with. I haven't got the courage to jump meself.

FRANK: I'm not throwing you overboard.

JIM: Do it. You might have a better chance of staying afloat if it's only yourself. Do it.

FRANK: I can't.

JIM: Do it.

FRANK: I haven't got the strength. Anyway. We're not taking on too much water. We're not going to drown.

JIM: What's going to happen to us, then?

FRANK: I allows we're going to freeze to death, Jim. I allows.

Long pause. Something gives the side of the boat a huge thump.

JIM: Stop rockin' the boat.

Something thumps the boat again. They hear the faint voice of JACK.

JACK: Haul me up, ye sons of mothers!

JIM: Shut up, Jack.

FRANK: Jack?

JACK: Haul me up, ye boat hogs!

FRANK: Jack. My God. Jim. Jim. It's Jack.

JACK: Haul me up, ye guards of Armageddon!

JIM: Where the frig is he?

JACK rises out of the water and gets his two arms over one side of the broken dory.

Don't tip us over.

JACK: I'll tip you over if you don't haul me aboard. Grab hold of me, Frank. My arms are done in.

FRANK: What's he floating on?

JACK: Grab hold of me, boys. This ride I hitched ain't sticking around for a tip.

They can barely manoeuvre but they manage to get him on board, almost capsizing in the process.

JIM: *(quietly, done in)* You were on the tail of a whale. He was on the tail of a whale. You were on the tail of a whale. The tail of a whale.

JACK: Look at her. Look at her. My beauty.

FRANK: I knows, now.

The two of them huddle around JACK. JACK *looks around and sees the state of the* Miss Tillie.

JACK: I should have stayed where I was.

JIM *laughs to himself.*

They hear whales all around them.

I was on a plank. I started to slip under. Slid into the water and brought up solid on something big. I slid right onto her back. I passed out for a while but she never dove. She never dove, lads.

The whales salute them in a great spray of water. They thump the boat.

(to the whale) So long, friend. I'll tell you what, lads. From now on, I'm a vegetarian.

FRANK: What? And give up salt beef?

JACK: Vegetarians can eat salt beef. They just don't eat meat or fish.

FRANK: Too bad they can't give us a tow.

JACK: We'll be charging price and a half for this shipment.

JIM: To who?

JACK: To the Pearly Gates by the look of ye two. Oh shit and shoe water, lads. I'm after losing my hat.

FRANK: What odds about your old hat.

JACK: That's the hat Al Capone gave me when we were drinking screech at the Hôtel Robért. Everyone says Capone left his hat in the hotel, but it wasn't his got left behind. It was mine. I was going to write it down in my memoirs.

JIM: If Capone is waiting for us at the Pearly Gates, he'd better not expect a cut of my share.

JACK: Jaysus, lads, we're not that bad off, are we? To be talking about the Pearly Gates.

Pause as they shiver and shake.

Oh. I see. I might have known Herself would never let me go.

FRANK: Jealous, see.

JACK: I should have known.

FRANK: All these years of smuggling out of Saint Pierre, too bad we never got to see it in daylight one time.

JIM: I hear it's a gorgeous place. Right French-like. They say the people are just the same as at home, except they're French. Got teeny little foreign cars. Little cobblestone streets.

FRANK: Mademoiselles so sweet looking it doesn't matter if they nag you or not 'cause you can't understand a frigging word they're saying.

JACK: No one is hateful.

FRANK: I hear the French pastries are nice.

JACK: Oh yes, the women are good to look at.

FRANK: I meant the French buns.

JACK: So did I.

Count to five. The men are freezing to death.

JIM: Ah well, b'ys. Ye had a good rum for the money.

JACK: I rode on the tail of a whale.

Pause. The men huddle together in the wreckage.

JIM: *(singing slowly, erratically.)* "Jack… was every… inch… a sailor."

JACK laughs with satisfaction.

"Five and…"

JACK: "Twenty years…"

JIM: "…a whaler. Jack was every inch a… rum runner…"

JACK: *(singing)* And he died upon the bright blue sea. Rockin' in the arms of Herself instead of a flesh-and-blood woman, but that's all right.

JIM: C'mon, Uncle Frank. Sing.

FRANK: Don't want to.

JIM: Why not?

FRANK: Just don't.

JIM: *(singing, erratically)* "The whale... went straight for... Baffin Bay, 'bout ninety knots an hour. And every time... he'd... blow a spray, he'd... send it in a shower."

A whale blows a spray next to the dory, but the men are too far gone to notice. There is a series of thumps against the boat.

"Oh, now... says Jack unto himself, I'll... see what he's about."

JACK: "He... got the whale all by the tail..."

Pause.

JIM: Cold, now. Ah, Lizzie.

Long pause. Ten count. A ray of sun strikes FRANK. He feels it. He looks up. He's too far gone to speak. He nudges JIM. JIM looks up.

Land.

JACK: Yes. But look over there.

JIM: It's the Mountie cutter. *(weakly)* Help! Help!

JACK: Now, shut up! Let's think on this.

JIM: Help! Help!

JACK: Shut up!

JIM: You shut up.

JACK: *Miss Tillie* here's got a bit of life left in her. If we can make it to shallow water, we can save the contraband.

JIM: No frigging way.

JACK: We made it this far.

JIM: Fuck off! Help! Help! Help!

FRANK reaches out his hand and grabs JIM by the arm.

Uncle Frank is dying, Jack. He's dying. Let him have his last words in peace. What is it, Uncle Frank? What are you trying to say?

Beat.

FRANK: Row.

JIM: Oh for God's sake.

FRANK: Row, Jim.

JIM: Row? There's too much drag on this thing.

JACK: We can do it.

JIM: You've got to be *codding* me!

FRANK: Jim. Try the planks.

JACK: Start rowing.

The sound of the Mountie cutter can be heard from off in the distance. JIM picks up a plank and starts to row. He throws a plank at JACK. The men can barely function. They row in jerky movements, like drunks.

JIM: Frig this. Signal the Mountie.

FRANK: No.

JACK: Next time, I'll put a backup motor on her. And two sets of oars, forward *and* aft.

JIM: Help! Help!

FRANK: I'm not going down for the greater good again, Jim.

JACK: Oh, you told him?

JIM: You knew?

JACK: Everyone knows except for you.

FRANK: Jack is too old to go down.

JACK: And I got a bad back.

FRANK: He can't go down. That leaves you. Now row if you don't want to be seeing that youngster of yours on visiting days in the pen.

JIM gives his uncle a murderous look and starts to row like the devil.

JIM: She's going to go tits up in a minute, I'm telling you.

JACK: We're close.

FRANK: Jim can rebuild her if we makes it.

JIM: Just 'cause I *can* salvage anything don't mean I will.

JACK: You fix her up and three of us will take her out for one last run, to work the kinks out.

JIM: No more smuggling. You said.

FRANK: Row!

JACK: I won't rest easy. Not until I know that *Miss Tillie* here can be seaworthy again.

FRANK: I'll give up the fibre blasted boat that floats on air.

JACK: *(sings)* "Jack was every inch a sailor. Five and twenty times a whaler."

Row, ye sons of heaven! Row, ye manly sailors!

JIM: Shut up, Jack.

JACK: "Jack was every inch a sailor. He was born upon the bright blue sea."

FRANK: One more run, Jim. We'll do it right next time.

JACK: Just to show we still got our spunk.

JIM: If I can rebuild her.

FRANK: I think that cop has us spotted.

JIM: Probably thinks we need help.

JACK: That's what's wrong with those fellows. They can't tell the difference between someone in distress and someone out for a jaunt.

The motor of the cutter is growing louder.

FRANK: If we can make it around that bend...

JIM: He's turning for us, all right.

JACK: Pull! How many times can a man say that he went out on the rum run of a lifetime? Pull! Faced down an angry Frenchman with a gun. Pull! Got rammed by a mysterious vessel. Pull! Swam with the whales. Pull! And floated home on a shitload of rum!

FRANK: *(to JIM)* Wait until your young fella makes *his* first run.

JIM: I'm only making one more run with ye. Out of the goodness of my heart. Only to make sure you're in a solid boat. And then I'm hanging up my bootlegs.

The sound of the cutter is muffled as they round the turn.

JACK: We're out of sight for a few seconds. He doesn't know *what* he's got in his sights. Hop over, Jim, pull us in behind them rocks.

JIM: Me? Why me? I hates the fucking water!

FRANK: For the spirits of the dead, my son. Show them your legs!

JIM: They'll haul me down!

JACK: Go for it, you sinner of salvation! Go for it!

FRANK: They can't haul you down! I'll keep you upright!

JIM: Oh merciful fuck.

FRANK: I can't wait to see my hateful wife again!

JIM: I can't!

JACK: One more run and I'm getting a store-bought missus!

JIM: I can't!

FRANK: Do it, son. Do it, son.

JIM: Well it's a rum for the money, and a two for the show, three to get ready and—

The Mountie cutter roars up behind them. The spotlight searches, then pins them in its sights. They freeze.

JACK: Bugger.

Blackout.

THE END

THE MONK

BY AIDEN FLYNN

ACKNOWLEDGEMENTS

I would like to acknowledge the Norstead Foundation for commissioning the original work that this published version is based on.

The Monk premiered as a workshop production at the Rabbittown Theatre, St. John's, on April 29, 2010, with the following cast and creative team:

Grenjar: Geoff Adams
The Monk: Aiden Flynn

Director: Aiden Flynn
Set design: Geoff Adams
Set construction: Mike Worthman

CHARACTERS

The Monk
Grenjar

THE SET

A suggestion of a rudimentary but solid Norse building—walls, roof, windows, and door. There is a central piece on a pivot. On one side there is a large, rugged carved crucifix. The other should indicate the bow of a Viking knarr. The central piece is rotated during the scene transitions to depict two settings, the chapel and Grenjar's boatshed. Smaller set pieces can be placed in the transitions as well. The fourth wall of the set is defined by a line of smooth, hand-sized beach rocks.

There should be a soundscape underneath the whole piece of sea rolling against a beach of rocks, a prevailing wind, and sea birds calling.

SCENE I

A small Christian chapel in a remote port, circa 1000 CE. A MONK *is working fussily around an altar, cleaning up after a service. He is young and diligent. These are the trappings of new Christianity and the chapel is sparse and rudimentary. He finally finishes, blesses himself. He also pulls out a small cloth that has something wrapped in it. He reads, but is obviously becoming tempted by the contents of the cloth. Again, after some time, he gives into temptation and opens the cloth to reveal a meagre piece of cake. He goes to the door. Seeing that nobody is about he goes back to his seat. He reverently puts the parchments aside and places the cake in front of him. He looks to the heavens. Says a short prayer. A look of agony comes over his face. He looks to the rugged crucifix behind him. He becomes resolved. He puts the cake aside, covers it, and retrieves his reading material. He begins to read again, and becomes engrossed in the material. Inadvertently, he reaches over and absently takes the piece of cake. He takes a bite, still engrossed in the text. He realizes what he has done and panic overtakes him. There is a knock on the door.*

MONK: *(with a full mouth)* One moment.

He hastily tries to cover up his indiscretion and chews furiously. The door opens. An old man enters. He is a bear of a man with a patch over one eye. He moves slowly but deliberately.

GRENJAR: Monk?

MONK: Yes, please, come in, come in.

The MONK *continues to right his wrong.*

GRENJAR: You're busy?

MONK: No, clearing up a little… reading.

GRENJAR: Is that so?

GRENJAR sniffs.

I smell cake.

MONK: NO! No.

GRENJAR: Hm. Too bad. A little cake might be a welcome change instead of that terrible bread you give out.

MONK: A pleasure of the flesh is not to be entertained in the walls of the sanctum.

GRENJAR: Daft.

MONK: Have you come to worship?

GRENJAR: What, your beat-up little man on the tree there? Don't be an idiot.

MONK: I see.

Pause.

Would you care to sit?

GRENJAR: Not really. I don't want to be seen in here. I'll just stand at the door here in case anyone happens by.

MONK: Very well.

Long pause.

GRENJAR is staring at the MONK's clothes.

GRENJAR: You *are* wearing women's clothes. They said you did.

MONK: Actually, these are the robes of my order. I have noticed that they are similar to the clothing your women wear.

GRENJAR: They are exactly the same. My late wife used to have a dress just like that.

MONK: I see.

GRENJAR: Of course, she filled it out better than you.

MONK: I would imagine.

Beat.

Not that I would imagine. I'm just saying that I'm sure your wife was… very beautiful.

GRENJAR: She was. I can have someone bring you some clothing for a man, if you want.

MONK: No, no. Thank you. I'm fine, really.

GRENJAR: Hm.

Pause.

MONK: Right. Well, you must have some cause to be here.

GRENJAR: Perhaps.

GRENJAR looks around the chapel. Takes it all in.

MONK: Grenjar, isn't it?

GRENJAR: That's my name, yes.

MONK: Yes, I think this is the first time we've met.

GRENJAR: It is.

MONK: Well, I'm glad to meet you. I hear a great deal about you from your daughter.

GRENJAR: I bet.

MONK: Pardon?

GRENJAR: You both talk about me behind my back?

MONK: Well, no… just…

GRENJAR: What does she say?

MONK: Nothing, really, certainly nothing bad.

GRENJAR: Hm.

GRENJAR continues to look around.

Well built.

MONK: Sorry?

GRENJAR: Your shed.

MONK: Chapel… actually.

GRENJAR: Solid.

MONK: Thanks.

GRENJAR: You're a skilled builder.

MONK: The order taught me.

GRENJAR: I see.

MONK: You're a boat builder, correct?

GRENJAR: I am.

MONK: I understand you are quite capable at it.

GRENJAR: I am.

MONK: Yes. Are you working on a vessel currently?

GRENJAR doesn't reply.

No... I suppose you're not, of course you're not.

GRENJAR: What d'y mean by that?

MONK: No, it's just that... I have heard around the village that you are... um... that you're not... well.

GRENJAR: Prattlers and scum. I should take my axe to their sculls.

MONK: Violence begets violence.

GRENJAR: What does that mean, now?

MONK: Simply that if you were to do something rash like that, a similar act may be returned in kind.

GRENJAR: By who? YOU!?

MONK: Certainly not, I meant...

GRENJAR: 'Cause if it's a fight you're looking for then I'm ready, willing, and able. And I tell you one thing, Thor would smile on me if I ever decided to separate that head of yours.

MONK: No, I would never dream of...

GRENJAR: Damn right you'd never dream, 'cause if you did dream you'd be dead... while you had your dream.

Pause. This threat is not working out so well.

'Cause I'd have killed ya.

MONK: I get it.

GRENJAR: Good.

Long uncomfortable pause.

MONK: Are you in need of some deliverance?

GRENJAR: What?

MONK: I know you're ill. I may not be able to remedy your ailment, but I can remedy a soul that needs salvation. Certainly one that may need... preparing.

GRENJAR: Preparing?

MONK: Yes, for the final "voyage," I suppose. Little joke there. Boats and all.

GRENJAR starts to laugh. The MONK starts to laugh. They laugh together.

Well, I guess we might be friends after all.

GRENJAR: Give over! I'm laughing at the thought of you trying to prepare me for anything. Let alone a "voyage."

GRENJAR's laughter builds to a crescendo that leads to a coughing fit.

MONK: Oh dear, can I get you some water?

The MONK gets a pitcher.

GRENJAR: Get away from me with that soft water that you pray over like a woman! I'll not be tricked by your weak magic.

MONK: This is not holy water, it's just… water.

GRENJAR: Give it here.

GRENJAR takes the water and swallows it heavily.

MONK: Better, yes?

GRENJAR: Hm.

GRENJAR hands back the pitcher.

MONK: I do wish you would sit down if you insist on staying.

GRENJAR: I'm fine.

MONK: You can bring the seat next to the door.

GRENJAR: Fine, fine. Give me the blasted chair.

The MONK retrieves a seat and brings it to GRENJAR, who sits.

You're not Norse.

MONK: No. I'm not.

GRENJAR: Where are your people from?

MONK: I'm Irish.

GRENJAR: Really. My grandfather did a lot of raiding and pillaging there. I think even a few monasteries, if I remember right.

MONK: Small world.

GRENJAR: It is.

MONK: How about you?

GRENJAR: From the old country.

MONK: How long have you been here?

GRENJAR: Since the beginning. I left when I was small boy. First Iceland. Then Greenland. Now here.

MONK: And you've never returned?

GRENJAR: No. I never shall. A shame. Some days I long to see it once more.

MONK: Yes.

GRENJAR: You've been here, what, a year?

MONK: About that.

GRENJAR: Why?

MONK: To set up this chapel, I suppose.

GRENJAR: Why here?

MONK: I was asked for. By the chieftain.

GRENJAR: Right! By his wife, you mean. She's the one who's all in love with the new Christ. She's got everyone all fooled into believing in the new god.

MONK: There might be some truth in that. I mean that his wife may have some influence. There's no foolery here, though.

GRENJAR: You've got my daughter fooled.

MONK: Yes, well, it's true, she's been coming here quite often. But I don't like the word "fooled" particularly.

GRENJAR: What would you call it?

MONK: Enlightened?

GRENJAR: Hm.

Pause.

I suppose she's the one who told you I'm sick.

MONK: She mentioned it, yes.

GRENJAR: She's the one who made me come here.

MONK: Made you?

GRENJAR: Yes… wait *(defensively)*… watch it, Monk! I'm my own man. I raised that girl by myself after her mother passed. And my house is my own.

MONK: I'm sorry, yes.

GRENJAR: I know she's a little… strong for a woman.

MONK: Perhaps a tad overbearing. She's been literally dragging others here for worship. I can see where she gets her strength.

Pause.

GRENJAR: You believe it?

MONK: Do I…?

GRENJAR: The story of your one god and the weakling on the tree.

MONK: I do.

GRENJAR: And you've come all the way to this village, for what?

MONK: To spread the word of Christ.

GRENJAR: It'll never catch on.

MONK: Most of the villagers are coming here quite regularly. I think you might be the last person I've met here, actually.

GRENJAR: You hear that the chieftain threatened them into coming here.

MONK: I've heard whispers.

GRENJAR: He threatened to cut their food.

MONK: Yes.

GRENJAR: Bastard.

MONK: Why didn't you come when he threatened everyone?

GRENJAR: Because he's full of it. I know that.

MONK: And your family suffered no consequences.

GRENJAR: No.

MONK: Brave.

GRENJAR: Hm. Don't try to flatter me, Monk.

MONK: I wouldn't dream of it.

GRENJAR: And don't think I'm here to fall to my knees like the rest of them. I'm only here to keep peace in my house. My daughter thinks that we shall suffer at the chieftain's hand if we do not convert.

MONK: I have to say, I don't like the sound of that.

GRENJAR: It's just a fad, anyway, your god.

MONK: You figure?

GRENJAR: Odin and Thor have many children who in turn have many children. You have the man on the tree. Odin will destroy him in battle.

MONK: You follow Odin.

GRENJAR: Yes.

MONK: And Thor, I would imagine.

GRENJAR: You know of Thor?

MONK: Yes, I find him quite...

GRENJAR: What?

MONK: Interesting.

GRENJAR: Interesting, please. All-powerful is more like it. Fierce and savage. Your god would be no match for him.

MONK: Christ has no intention of fighting Odin, or anyone for that matter.

GRENJAR: A god who will not fight? What's the point?

MONK: To love.

GRENJAR: What?

MONK: Love.

GRENJAR: You're not serious, are you?

MONK: Quite.

GRENJAR: If I had known that I might have given you the benefit of the doubt. You mean this is all about being able to take more women?

MONK: No. No, you misunderstand...

GRENJAR: 'Cause if I'd known that I'd be here every day. How many women do you take?

MONK: None. You don't understand...

GRENJAR: None. Are you one of those kind without your manhood?

MONK: NO!

GRENJAR: Well, what's your problem? Love as many as you can, I'd say. And if that is what happens in here, why can't my daughter be taken by a man herself? She looks good enough. It's time she was taken by someone.

MONK: Oh my God, I mean—*(to the crucifx)* sorry, forgive me, please— no, let me explain.

GRENJAR: What?

MONK: When I say love, I mean love in a more profound way. To understand one another, and to help each other. To care for each other and not fight, but listen, and to look past the hurtful things that others may do.

Another long pause.

Love thy neighbour as you would yourself, essentially.

GRENJAR: WHAT?

MONK: Not in the way *you* think. Like I just explained.

GRENJAR: Let me tell you what I believe in, Monk.

MONK: Sure.

GRENJAR: Honour. And protecting what's yours. My gods will exact revenge on anyone who will cross them. Not right away. Only a slave takes revenge right away. But a fool never takes revenge at all. When the time is right. Maybe not even in my lifetime. But those who bear my name will do so in their days. Maybe my sons, or the sons of my sons. They will maintain honour at any price. That's what happens if anyone crosses me.

MONK: You don't have any sons.

GRENJAR: Believe me, my daughter can be son enough.

MONK: Amen.

Pause.

That all sounds a little exhausting.

GRENJAR: Nobody said honour was easy, Monk. And as for helping one another, I don't need the man on the tree for that. I'm farmer class. We all help each other. But you and him, you'd both have me bow down to my slave. My daughter prattles on about your words on slaves.

MONK: Well, not bow down, exactly.

GRENJAR: But you think we should be equals.

MONK: Well…

GRENJAR laughs.

GRENJAR: Good luck in trying to convince people to not keep slaves. How would anything get done?

MONK: Let's agree to disagree on the slavery. And love for that matter.

GRENJAR: Let's.

Pause.

MONK: You mentioned honour. How about honour thy father?

GRENJAR: Hm?

MONK: I think your daughter sent you here today.

GRENJAR: I was afraid she might quarter me in my sleep if I didn't. She's quite mad.

MONK: That we *can* agree on, I suppose.

GRENJAR: She wants me to become a Christian.

MONK: I see.

GRENJAR: I'd rather this cough kill me right now in your shed.

MONK: Grenjar… may I call you Grenjar?

GRENJAR: I suppose.

MONK: I realize you are a man of your convictions.

GRENJAR: That's right.

MONK: What can I possibly do for you? Why are you here?

Long pause.

Can I help you, in some way?

GRENJAR: I want to make sure my daughter is content when I'm gone.

MONK: Of course.

GRENJAR: She doesn't have a husband. I fear that's my fault.

MONK: I don't think she needs one, necessarily. She's quite resourceful.

GRENJAR: I'm worried that the chieftain and his cow of a wife will mistreat her when I'm gone because of me.

Pause.

And I'm worried that her anger for me will live when I am dead. I am worried that if I don't follow your god and forget mine, that she will not speak my name.

MONK: I see.

GRENJAR: I have no sons. And my name is all I have. If she doesn't speak it, then the roots of my family will rot and die, and my tree will fall. But if I turn my back on Thor, there will be no seat for me in the heavens. I will not sit with my fathers. Where do the Christians live in the next life?

MONK: With Christ. We will walk alongside the perfection of the Lord.

GRENJAR *looks to the crucifix.*

GRENJAR: What makes him so perfect?

MONK: His perpetual light, wisdom. His love.

Pause. GRENJAR *is not entirely impressed.*

GRENJAR: What about mead? Does he enjoy a horn of mead once in a while?

MONK: I… I don't think so.

GRENJAR: Does he sing? Gamble? What does he do for fun?

MONK: Um… well… he… I'm not quite sure.

GRENJAR: I know Thor laughs at me now for even having this conversation.

MONK: Perhaps I can speak with your daughter. Tell her of your concerns.

GRENJAR: You are braver than you look.

MONK: I can visit her later today if you wish.

GRENJAR: I'm not sure if that's such a good idea. Perhaps you should leave well enough alone. I'll tell her that I didn't come here today. That I was in my boatshed. At least then she'll take it out on me, and you might live through the night.

MONK: No, please, I insist. Christ smiles on those who suffer in his name.

GRENJAR: He'll be smiling all over you then. I'll be on my way.

MONK: Peace be with you.

GRENJAR: Not when I get home it won't.

GRENJAR goes to leave.

Is your man really going to be sore with you if you eat the rest of that cake?

The MONK reacts. He's caught.

MONK: Oh. I'll only find out when I meet him, I guess.

GRENJAR: I'd eat it then. I'm sure he must have other business than just looking after you and your weakness for cake.

MONK: Perhaps. But I will offer this sacrifice up for my sins.

GRENJAR: Daft.

GRENJAR exits.

The MONK returns to his reading. He looks to the crucifix. And finishes the cake. He enjoys it briefly, and then a look of guilt sweeps over his face. Blackout.

SCENE II

GRENJAR's boatshed. The hull of an impressive knarr takes up most of the space.

GRENJAR is working with a piece of wood, carving something that needs to be precise. He pores over it, taking care in each stroke of his knife over the wood. He puts it down and tries to rub the ache out of his fingers and looks at the knarr. He picks up the knife again and starts to carve the wood once more. He is distracted by the knarr. The knife skips off the wood and cuts his hand. It's a deep cut and there is a quick rush of blood from the wound. He scrambles to find something to cover the cut. But he is still drawn to the knarr. He looks at the blood that has now covered his hand. He goes to the unfinished maidenhead. He raises the wounded hand to the boat.

GRENJAR: Bone to bone,
blood to blood,
limb to limb,
such as they belong together.

A knock at the door.

Who's that?

MONK: *(off stage)* Grenjar?

GRENJAR: Monk?

MONK: Yes.

Pause.

GRENJAR: What do you want?

MONK: May I come in?

GRENJAR: No.

MONK: No?

GRENJAR: You heard me. No.

Pause.

MONK: Please?

GRENJAR sighs reluctantly and goes to the door. He throws the latch.

GRENJAR: What is it?

MONK: I thought I might pay a visit.

GRENJAR: Why?

MONK: Just to be friendly, I suppose.

GRENJAR: Hm.

MONK: May I come in?

GRENJAR: I do not allow anyone in here.

MONK: Oh.

Pause.

I guess I'll be leaving.

Pause.

Well... see ya.

He turns and goes.

GRENJAR *goes back to his workbench. He tends to his hand. He tries to work the piece of wood once again but the wound is too painful.*

A slight knock on the door.

(off stage) Grenjar?

GRENJAR *huffs and goes to the door, opens it, and returns to his seat. Starts to hack.*

GRENJAR: I see I'll get no work done this day.

MONK: I'm sorry, I didn't mean to... it's just that...

GRENJAR: *(coughing)* Come in and sit, if you must.

MONK: Thanks, I really won't take up much of your time, I...

GRENJAR: *(coughing)* Sit.

The MONK *takes a seat on the other side of the shed.* GRENJAR *sits at his workbench. His coughing subsides.*

Silence.

What do you want, Monk?

MONK: I've been thinking a lot about our conversation earlier... oh... your hand.

GRENJAR: It's nothing.

MONK: It looks serious.

GRENJAR: It's fine.

MONK: Can I help you with it?

GRENJAR: No.

MONK: I think you may need it sutured. I'm actually quite good with a needle and thread.

GRENJAR: What a shock.

MONK: Please, let me see.

GRENJAR offers the hand.

I think it needs to be sewn. Do you have a...

GRENJAR: Over there.

The MONK retrieves a needle. He puts the needle in a pot that is boiling over a fire.

MONK: How did you do this?

GRENJAR: I work.

MONK: Right.

The MONK looks to the knarr.

Did you build this?

Silence.

Of course you did. It's beautiful.

Silence.

Did you build it all by yourself?

GRENJAR: Yes!

MONK: Yes, sorry, I didn't mean to imply...

GRENJAR: Why are you here, Monk?

MONK: I was hoping we could talk some more.

GRENJAR: About what?

MONK: I was hoping... you could tell me more about... well... Thor?

GRENJAR: Why?

The MONK looks to the needle.

MONK: That should be ready now. You might want to clean up that hand before I start...

The MONK goes and prepares the needle. GRENJAR cleans the wound.

GRENJAR: Why do you want to know about my gods?

MONK: I thought it might help me...

GRENJAR: How?

MONK: I was thinking about what you said, about the chieftain. The way he's been threatening the people of the port.

GRENJAR: And...

MONK: And, it makes me a little uncomfortable, knowing that these measures are being taken to bring people to the chapel.

GRENJAR: Hm.

MONK: I thought, if I knew more about what you believe, people could come with a more... open heart. Perhaps I could understand you a little better.

GRENJAR: I am not a complicated man.

MONK: I don't know about that.

The MONK takes GRENJAR's hand.

This is going to hurt. Perhaps you might want to take a drink, or something, if you have one.

GRENJAR: No.

MONK: All right.

The MONK goes to work.

Three or four should do it.

GRENJAR shows his discomfort.

Good?

GRENJAR: Just finish it, Monk.

MONK: How long did it take you to build it? The boat?

GRENJAR: Not long.

MONK: Really? You are as skilled as they say. Are you a good boatman? Pilot, I mean.

GRENJAR: Fair. My father was a great boatman.

MONK: That so? I'm a pretty good hand it myself.

GRENJAR snorts.

That surprises you?

GRENJAR: Very much.

MONK: Perhaps I could show you sometime.

GRENJAR: Hm.

MONK: A lot of the brothers in my order are skilled navigators and quite good at piloting smaller vessels.

GRENJAR: Why would they need to know that?

MONK: Our work requires a fair bit of travel.

GRENJAR: I see.

MONK: I helped pilot the vessel that brought me here.

GRENJAR: A difficult voyage.

MONK: Challenging, yes.

GRENJAR: Where else have you been?

MONK: Many places. This is the farthest I've ventured.

GRENJAR: My father took me to the south, when I was a child. To purchase slaves.

The MONK is unsettled by this.

MONK: I see.

GRENJAR: Warm waters there.

MONK: Yes.

Pause.

I think I'm pretty much done here.

GRENJAR *looks at the wound.*

GRENJAR: Good job.

MONK: Thanks. Not completely useless, am I?

GRENJAR: Hm.

MONK: I have something at the chapel that would keep it clean and keep it from getting infected.

GRENJAR: No.

MONK: Really, it's no trouble…

GRENJAR: No, Monk.

MONK: Fair enough. You should tie this tight around the cut.

The MONK hands him some cloth.

Pause.

GRENJAR: Would you care for some food? I have cake.

MONK: Well…

GRENJAR: You're in my shed now, Monk, no need to worry about the beat-up man on the tree.

MONK: He lives everywhere.

GRENJAR: Not here, Monk. Have some cake.

GRENJAR offers him a piece of cake from his bag.

MONK: Thank you.

They eat.

It's quite good.

GRENJAR: My daughter made it.

MONK: She's a good baker.

GRENJAR: One thing she took from her dead mother.

MONK: How long has your wife been gone?

GRENJAR: A long time. Many years.

Pause.

MONK: Did your daughter know her mother?

GRENJAR: No. Too young.

MONK: Pity.

Pause.

You miss her.

GRENJAR: What?

MONK: Your wife.

GRENJAR: Why do you talk this way?

MONK: What do you mean?

GRENJAR: You talk to me...

MONK: Yes?

GRENJAR: ...like a woman.

MONK: What does that mean?

GRENJAR: You talk soft.

MONK: Is that so?

GRENJAR: You speak to me like a...

MONK: ...friend?

GRENJAR: Hm.

MONK: We could be friends.

GRENJAR: I don't think so.

MONK: Why?

Pause.

GRENJAR: You are a strange man, Monk.

MONK: Sorry.

Pause.

You know, I went to see her... your daughter... before I came here.

GRENJAR: What?

MONK: Like I said I would.

GRENJAR: You shouldn't have.

MONK: It was fine, really.

GRENJAR: I told you not to.

MONK: I know.

GRENJAR: Why did you?

MONK: You seemed troubled.

GRENJAR: You haven't seen trouble. Wait until I get home.

MONK: I told her of your concerns.

GRENJAR: What!? I told you that man to man. Perhaps I should have remembered your little dress.

MONK: She still wants you to come to the chapel.

GRENJAR: No.

MONK: I told her I didn't think it was a great idea.

GRENJAR: Really? Why? Your job is to convert us, isn't it?

MONK: I... I don't know... I don't think so.

GRENJAR: You're starting to confuse me, Monk.

Pause.

MONK: Would you tell me about Thor?

GRENJAR: No, I'm busy.

MONK: You should let that wound heal.

GRENJAR: It's nothing.

GRENJAR goes to pick up a tool, which proves difficult.

MONK: Just for a day or so.

GRENJAR: You might be right.

MONK: So... Thor.

GRENJAR: What?

MONK: Could you tell me about him?

GRENJAR: What's to tell, Monk? He is strong, wise... to be feared.

MONK: Fear. Is that why you follow him? Because you fear him?

GRENJAR is a little taken back.

GRENJAR: Yes. In a way, yes.

MONK: What do you fear?

GRENJAR: He can take from me... everything. Leave me with...

MONK: ...nothing?

GRENJAR: Yes.

MONK: Why would he do that?

GRENJAR: If I displease him.

MONK: I see. Displease him how?

GRENJAR: Live cowardly.

MONK: What does that mean?

GRENJAR: To live afraid. Afraid of others. Afraid of the world.

MONK: I see. How do you serve him then?

GRENJAR: I work. I build things in his name.

MONK: Like this vessel.

GRENJAR: Yes.

MONK: And that pleases him?

GRENJAR: Yes.

MONK: Interesting. Similar, really.

GRENJAR: To what?

MONK: To my belief.

GRENJAR: Hm.

GRENJAR *starts to cough.*

Broth?

MONK: Thank you, yes.

The MONK *prepares some broth.*

I work to serve my god as well.

GRENJAR: What work? I see you tending a garden and reading mostly. That's not work.

MONK: You don't think so?

GRENJAR: No, Monk, I do not.

MONK: To each his own.

Pause.

Do you pray to Thor?

GRENJAR: What do you mean?

MONK: Um… pray… speak to him.

GRENJAR: Speak to him?

MONK: Ask him for guidance?

GRENJAR: Do you speak to the White Christ?

MONK: I do.

GRENJAR: Does he speak back?

MONK: In a way.

GRENJAR: What way?

MONK: He speaks through my actions, reasoning, compassion, I guess.

GRENJAR: What does that mean?

MONK: It's a little hard to explain.

GRENJAR *laughs.*

What?

GRENJAR: Your god has no voice. I've seen him in your little shed. He hangs from his tree and looks sad.

MONK: That's not really the case, he…

GRENJAR: The voice of my gods speak constantly. The oceans roll, the wind howls over barrens and through trees, and the skies open wide, especially in this land.

MONK: That's true.

GRENJAR: Odin and Thor live alongside me. We don't speak. I have no need to speak to them. I listen. And I take whatever they choose to give me. Bounty or misfortune.

MONK: Why do you think your people have stopped believing in their gods?

GRENJAR: I told you why. The chieftain.

MONK: Is that the only reason?

GRENJAR: Yes. Why else?

MONK: I don't know… people seem to be uplifted by the words I speak to them.

GRENJAR: Really? What do you say?

MONK: Well, for instance, yesterday, before you came by, I was reading from the words of the saint that I follow, St. Anthony. St. Anthony was the first monk. He lived in Egypt. He dedicated his life to solitude in service to God. I told the people how similar they were to St. Anthony. Dedicating their lives to their work in this remote, isolated corner of the world. I told them how God smiles on them for their conviction to maintaining lives in quiet reverence and solitude. They seemed to like it.

GRENJAR: Your god smiles on those who are alone?

MONK: Well, not just those who are alone...

GRENJAR: Is that why you came here? To be alone.

The MONK is taken aback a bit.

MONK: I suppose.

Pause.

I guess I should be going.

GRENJAR: All right.

MONK: Thanks... for the broth... and cake... and for speaking with me.

GRENJAR: Hm.

MONK: Take care of your hand.

GRENJAR: Yes.

The MONK turns to go.

Monk?

MONK: Yes?

GRENJAR: What did my daughter say to you? Why did you come here?

MONK: She said... she said that she really wanted me to convince you to come with her to the chapel. I guess I came to...

GRENJAR: ...to what?

MONK: To see your chapel, I guess.

Pause.

Bye.

The MONK *leaves.* GRENJAR *finishes his broth. He looks at his injured hand and tries to work with his left hand. Blackout.*

SCENE III

The chapel. The MONK *is poring over text. He hears* GRENJAR's *cough in the distance. He goes and prepares a seat for him at the door.*

GRENJAR: *(off stage)* Monk?

MONK: Yes, Grenjar.

Pause.

Come in and sit.

GRENJAR: *(off stage)* Is there anyone in there?

MONK: Just me and the man on the tree.

GRENJAR *enters.*

GRENJAR: Busy?

MONK: I was just reading a…

GRENJAR: Not busy. Good.

MONK: Well, two visits from Grenjar the Enigmatic in two days. What a treat. Please, sit.

GRENJAR: No.

MONK: Why?

GRENJAR: I don't want…

MONK: …to be seen in here. Right, I don't think I'm expecting anyone, it's quite early.

GRENJAR: Fine.

GRENJAR *sits.*

MONK: I actually have something for you.

GRENJAR: What?

MONK: Wait here.

The MONK *leaves.*

GRENJAR gets up, looks around, looks at the text. The MONK re-enters.

Grenjar?

GRENJAR: What is that?

MONK: Something from the garden. It might help with the cough.

The MONK hands GRENJAR a small sack.

GRENJAR: No need for this.

MONK: I know. It might subside the hack a little though.

GRENJAR: Hm.

MONK: How are you feeling?

GRENJAR: I feel fine.

MONK: You don't look well. Tired.

GRENJAR: I've been working.

MONK: Have you been sleeping?

GRENJAR: Who can sleep? My daughter causes me grief every waking second it seems with her talk of this blasted chapel and the White Christ.

MONK: I see.

GRENJAR: She wants me to be buried as a Christian. Not only does she have me dead before my time, but she wants me put in the ground like a turnip.

MONK: I'm sure she is concerned for your well-being.

GRENJAR: She is concerned for her own. She wants to be held in favour with that cow of a woman that the chieftain married.

MONK: I see.

GRENJAR: So I go to my shed and build my boat. It's the only thing that makes sense in this world anymore.

MONK: You should really take it easy. I'm sure there is no rush on the boat.

GRENJAR: Hm.

Pause.

MONK: And how's the hand?

GRENJAR: Fine.

MONK: Right, well, I hope the medicine helps.

GRENJAR: Hm.

The MONK points to the text.

MONK: You were reading when I came in.

GRENJAR: I don't read.

MONK: Right.

GRENJAR: I just thought I might see what it is that wastes your time in here.

MONK: This is it.

GRENJAR: What does it say?

MONK: Writings on St. Anthony. The saint I was telling you about yesterday.

GRENJAR: I do like the drawings.

MONK: Really?

GRENJAR: Yes.

MONK: Well, the drawings are mine.

GRENJAR: Really.

MONK: That's right.

GRENJAR examines them more closely.

GRENJAR: They're good.

MONK: Thanks.

GRENJAR: I like the serpent.

MONK: Yes, well it's a snake in the desert. That's St. Anthony.

GRENJAR: Why did you draw it?

MONK: I was inspired, I guess. God's work.

GRENJAR: Your work. God had nothing to do with it.

Pause.

Hm. What's he doing?

MONK: It depicts his choice to live in solitude.

GRENJAR: And the serpent?

MONK: Oh… it's supposed to compare his struggle to that of Christ. *(realizing)* You don't know… right… Christ went to the desert and was tempted by Satan. It's supposed to draw an analogy to St. Anthony.

GRENJAR: Who's Satan?

MONK: He is the… you really don't…? No, you wouldn't… uh… well, Satan is a fallen angel. He took on the form of a snake in the story.

GRENJAR: Hm. Like Loki.

MONK: Loki?

GRENJAR: He can turn into different animals. He's a real character. So, you like Satan as well?

MONK: No.

GRENJAR: Why not? You draw him so well.

MONK: Because… he's… evil.

GRENJAR: Evil?

MONK: Yes.

GRENJAR: How?

MONK: He is… chaos. He causes sorrow and misery.

GRENJAR: I see.

GRENJAR *looks at the drawing again.*

What's the problem with that?

MONK: What… it's… it's wrong.

GRENJAR: Hm.

Pause.

MONK: You don't agree.

GRENJAR: I don't.

MONK: How can you say that?

GRENJAR: Because the world is full of sorrow and misery.

MONK: Right. Don't you think that's wrong?

GRENJAR: I doesn't matter what I think. It is. It won't change.

MONK: It matters and it can change. You can change things with your daughter.

GRENJAR: I cannot. She wants me to forget my ways. I will not do it. If her anger subsides, that will be the way of things. I cannot change that.

MONK: But...

GRENJAR: Yes?

MONK: ...good point.

GRENJAR: Changing things is important to you?

MONK: What?

GRENJAR: That's why you're here.

MONK: In a way.

GRENJAR: You've changed things a great deal.

MONK: Yes.

GRENJAR: You don't seem happy with it.

MONK: I'm not particularly.

GRENJAR: Then stop.

MONK: I can't.

GRENJAR: Why?

MONK: Because, I have a job to do here.

GRENJAR: Work is important. One must do his work.

MONK: Yes.

GRENJAR: One must be eager in his work though, to do it well.

MONK: Must one?

GRENJAR: You seem to have lost your eagerness.

MONK: I feel like I'm part of something...

GRENJAR: ...wrong.

MONK: Yes.

GRENJAR: You feel tempted to stop?

MONK: Yes.

Pause.

GRENJAR: Then stop.

MONK: I made a promise. To the order. To the chieftain. To myself. And to God.

GRENJAR: A heavy burden. You seem to have carried out your promise to your order.

MONK: Maybe.

GRENJAR: The chieftain is a bully and can go hang. As well as his ugly wife.

MONK: Uh...

GRENJAR: You don't need to answer that. So it seems your dilemma is with you... and the White Christ.

MONK: Seems you might be right.

GRENJAR: Can I speak my mind to you?

MONK: Uh... yeah...

GRENJAR: Do not live your life according to the will of the man on the tree. Live your life according to what makes sense to your life here. We are given no time here. Mountains are given time. Oceans are given time. The earth and the sky are given time. We live for a second. I live my life in respect to the gods and their work, but not in service. I am no slave. I pity no slave. If you do not wish to be one, kill your master. Be your own man.

MONK: Hm.

Pause.

GRENJAR: I have said too much.

MONK: No. No.

GRENJAR: Forgive me.

MONK: Not necessary. You have given me a great deal to consider.

GRENJAR: Hm.

Pause.

MONK: Can I speak to you?

GRENJAR: You can.

MONK: I have been a monk for a very short time. Perhaps ten years. Do you know what I did before that? I was a slave trader. I came from a wealthy family. I wanted for nothing. One day, I was with my father in lands to the east. He had taken a woman in a trade. She had a daughter. I could see the look in the little girl's eyes. Like I had taken… everything from her… left her with… nothing. I sailed with that woman for days. And I saw her. For the first time I had seen a person for their real worth. I joined my order of brothers shortly after, and abandoned my old life. And I read. And I learned skills, skills that I could offer to Christ. And I vowed to change my life and the world in his name. And I decided to do this in isolation. To cut myself off from people in order to try and appreciate them more. And I came here. And now…

GRENJAR: What, Monk?

MONK: Now I feel like I did as a slave trader. That my life is not my own. That nobody's life is their own. I've done that. I've caused that. But…

He looks at GRENJAR.

GRENJAR: Hm?

MONK: But not you.

GRENJAR: Hm.

MONK: You're the only one I haven't hurt.

GRENJAR: No one is hurt. Just…

MONK: …fooled.

GRENJAR: Maybe.

Pause.

MONK: I don't know what to do anymore.

GRENJAR *looks around the chapel.*

GRENJAR: You are good with your hands. I've seen that.

MONK: Thanks.

GRENJAR: And you are not lazy.

MONK: No, I guess not.

GRENJAR: I am not well.

MONK: I know.

GRENJAR: I've come to ask your help.

MONK: Really.

GRENJAR: I fear I will not finish my boat in time.

MONK: In time for what.

GRENJAR: I'm building it for a funeral.

MONK: I see.

GRENJAR: Will you help me finish it?

MONK: Um…

GRENJAR: Well?

MONK: …yes… yes, I will. I'd be honoured.

GRENJAR: You can come tomorrow?

MONK: Yes.

When you are ready then.

Are you sure?

No answer.

Of course you are.

GRENJAR: You have a good mind and hands for drawing.

MONK: Yes.

GRENJAR: Maybe you can use that mind to think about a maidenhead for the boat.

MONK: Yes, I could do that.

GRENJAR: Tomorrow, then.

GRENJAR goes to leave.

MONK: You said the boat was for a funeral.

GRENJAR: That's right.

MONK: Is it… for yours?

GRENJAR: That's right.

MONK: So the boat is kind of a… coffin.

GRENJAR: *(smiling)* That's right. Tomorrow, Monk.

GRENJAR leaves. The MONK puts away his writings. Blackout.

SCENE IV

The MONK is dressed in work attire and works at the hull of the boat. GRENJAR is seated and is sharpening a tool. They have been talking for some time.

GRENJAR: All the gods were destroyed in the Ragnarok.

MONK: Right… they were all destroyed in this battle.

GRENJAR: That's right. And Loki fought on the side of the giants.

MONK: He betrayed the gods.

GRENJAR: He did. They never saw it coming.

MONK: So you're telling me that all the gods are gone.

GRENJAR: Of course.

MONK: Then what was all this about "my gods live in the trees, and the water, and the wind."

GRENJAR: They do.

MONK: Sorry, it's been a week and I still don't understand.

GRENJAR: Take it on faith, Monk.

MONK: I suppose I'll have to.

GRENJAR: You've done good work on the hull. The seams are tight.

MONK: I think I should look at the port side near the gunwales again.

GRENJAR: No need.

MONK: I think they could be better.

GRENJAR: I like that you're careful, but the work that high above the waterline won't make a difference. Not for our purpose.

MONK: I guess. Do you really intend to burn this beautiful creation when it is done? It seems like such a shame.

GRENJAR: I will be laid to rest in the boat, pulled out to sea, and then the boat will be set alight. Like Balder.

MONK: And will you return, like Balder did after Ragnarok?

GRENJAR: Don't worry, Monk, I will not.

Pause.

What will we do with the bow? How will we decorate it?

MONK: I have some ideas. I could carve a snake possibly.

GRENJAR: Like the one that poisoned Loki. Like your Satan.

MONK: Yes. I could also…

The MONK hesitates.

GRENJAR: What?

MONK: I could also carve it in the likeness of your wife.

GRENJAR: Hm. She was a goddess.

Pause.

MONK: Have you spoken with your daughter about me coming here to help you?

GRENJAR: No.

MONK: You said that you would.

GRENJAR: I know. I'm waiting for the right time.

GRENJAR goes into a coughing fit.

MONK: You might want to do it soon.

GRENJAR: You too, eh, Monk? You have me dead as well.

MONK: No, Grenjar.

GRENJAR: You do.

MONK: I just think you should try to reconcile with her. Before it's too late.

GRENJAR: She still insists on your Christian burial for me.

MONK: I know.

Pause.

GRENJAR: What will you do, Monk?

MONK: What do you mean?

GRENJAR: When I die.

MONK: I will... I will mourn you. But who's to say you will die before me. You've been working me like a whipped mule.

GRENJAR: Will you bury me, Monk?

MONK: It's not really my decision. Besides, that's why we're building this boat, isn't it?

GRENJAR: You know that I really will have no say. My daughter will insist on the Christian burial and my wishes will be denied.

MONK: That's why you should talk with her.

GRENJAR: She will not listen.

MONK: You could reason with her.

GRENJAR: No. She thinks I'm senile and foolish. She will do as she intends and please the chieftain.

MONK: Perhaps we could go see him.

GRENJAR: No.

MONK: Why?

GRENJAR: You still insist on change.

MONK: But...

GRENJAR: There is no change here, Monk. Only choice. What choice will you make?

MONK: It is... too much.

Pause.

GRENJAR: You are right. It is too much for you.

Pause.

MONK: Tell me another tale of Thor.

GRENJAR: I've told you many this week.

MONK: Surely there is another.

GRENJAR: I am too tired to fight with you. Put some broth on.

The MONK attends to the fire.

You will like this, it's about a snake.

When Thor reached the edge of the battlefield for Ragnarok, he saw many foes. Giants in numbers like rocks on the beach. Creatures fierce and dangerous. But the greatest foe was the world serpent, Jormungand. Thor had faced the serpent many times. He had smashed it with his hammer when he went to retrieve the kettle for Aegir's feast, remember?

MONK: I do.

GRENJAR: When Thor looked across the plains of Vigrid and saw the serpent, he tightened his belt of strength and gripped Mjolnir in his fist. He raced across the plain and locked in combat with the snake. For an eternity he grappled with the demon. At last both combatants killed each other. But they knew they would. They know they will. The outcome has been and will forever be laid out for them. They succumbed to the fates.

GRENJAR puts down the tool he has been working with.

We all must face our fate.

The MONK hands him broth.

MONK: It's hot.

GRENJAR pauses and looks at the knarr.

GRENJAR: Bone to bone,
blood to blood,
limb to limb,
such as they belong together.

MONK: What is that?

GRENJAR: A prayer, I suppose.

MONK: It's beautiful.

GRENJAR: Monk?

MONK: Yes?

GRENJAR: I will go with my daughter to your chapel. I will listen to your words.

MONK: What? No.

GRENJAR: It's what you wish. It's what she wishes.

MONK: But, I don't wish it.

GRENJAR: It's why you came. To do your work, and I will not stand in your way anymore. But you must do something for me.

MONK: What?

GRENJAR: You must leave. You must answer to your own fate. I want you to use the boat.

MONK: But your... I can't.

GRENJAR: You will. Leave and pilot this vessel. You should be able to handle it by yourself. You might need to check those seams, though.

MONK: Where would I go?

GRENJAR: I don't know. But your fate does not lie here. You should go. And be with people again. Your work is done.

MONK: What would I do?

GRENJAR: You have great skill. Use it to satisfy yourself, and nobody else.

MONK: I don't know about this.

GRENJAR is starting to cough more.

GRENJAR: Go now to your shed. I will talk with my daughter. We will meet you at your... chapel tomorrow morning. You can make me a Christian.

Pause.

MONK: I'll go.

GRENJAR: I want you to have this.

GRENJAR pulls a pendant out from under his shirt.

Thor's hammer. Looks a little like the tree your man is on.

MONK: I can't take this.

GRENJAR: You can. A gift for your help on my boat.

MONK: Grenjar...

GRENJAR: No more talk now, Monk. Tomorrow.

The MONK *leaves.* GRENJAR *sits. His breathing is laboured. He closes his eyes. Blackout.*

SCENE V

The MONK *is preparing for a ceremony. He is careful but is not happy in this work. He finally finishes and sits. Long and uncomfortable silence. He realizes he is wearing the pendant that* GRENJAR *gave him. He takes it off reverently and puts it in a pouch on his belt. He continues to wait. He goes to a window, obviously looking for someone who is not coming. Back to his seat. He is noticeably distressed now. He goes to the door. He stands in the door and is becoming more upset. As he stares out the door we hear the rise of the wind and the surf. He looks skyward and the sound of the seabirds increases. The sounds swell and the lights black out.*

SCENE VI

The sound of the swollen outdoor state continues into this scene. As the lights come up we are at neither the boatshed nor the Chapel. We are at a gravesite. The MONK *carefully takes the rocks that define the fourth wall and reworks them into a rectangular shape the size of a grave. As he is arranging the stones he is going through ancient Christian burial rights in Latin. When he is finished placing the rocks he stands over them. He performs the sign of the cross over the grave and finishes his prayer. The lights go to black and the sounds of the wind, sea, and birds subside to their previous level.*

SCENE VII

Intense front lights depicting two large doors opening on an early morning come up on the set. We are in the boatshed. The MONK *stands and looks at the knarr. He has a significant bag over his shoulder, which he puts down. He takes out Thor's hammer from where it was stored in his belt pouch and puts it on. The* MONK *throws the bag over his shoulder again and grabs a tow line from the front of the boat.*

MONK: Bone to bone,
blood to blood,
limb to limb,
such as they belong together.

The MONK *looks to the knarr once more and digs in his heels to start pulling the boat out of the shed. He blesses himself, and as he pulls, the lights go to black.*

Curtain.

THE END

HAIL

BY EDWARD RICHE

Hail was first produced by RCA Theatre Company at LSPU Hall, St. John's, from May 26 to June 5, 2011. It featured the following cast and creative team:

Len: Aiden Flynn
Paul: Brad Hodder
Gerry: Brian Marler
Danny: Robert Joy

Director: Charlie Tomlinson

CHARACTERS

Len: early to mid forties
Gerry: early to mid forties
Paul: early to mid forties
Danny: early to mid fifties

The ethnicity of any and all is not important. There are class differences between the men that will become evident in the text.

SETTING

A small city, under one million souls, in the first decade of the twenty-first century.

ACT ONE

A small industrial garage—dusk.

Heavy standing power tools have been pushed together and aside against the wall upstage right. There are a couple of wooden crates, a couple of metal chairs. There is a workbench with a few scattered hand tools of mysterious utility. Upstage centre (farther downstage and centre than the unused power tools) is a table and chairs covered in a tarp. There are tall windows stage left, shuttered from within. There are two work lights, bulbs in metal cages hanging from above, as yet unlit. A large lamp, cheesy faux-Tiffany perhaps, unlit, hangs from a cord over the tarp-covered table.

The only light comes from an exit sign above a door, left, and a thin beam between the shutters on the windows. A man, GERRY, *anxiously paces.* GERRY *is dressed casually, in jeans, a button-up shirt, and a windbreaker. He is non-descript.*

GERRY walks to the door. There he brushes his hand against the wall in search of a light switch. He finds and flips a switch. A fluorescent tube comes on above. GERRY *opens the shutters on the two big windows. This allows a blue light from outside to enter the room.*

Car headlights sweep over the open windows and illuminate the room and GERRY's face. The lights return to the windows and light the room but cease their motion. A car engine is heard outside. It idles for a moment. The car lights are extinguished and, soon after, the engine. Outside a car door opens and closes. The door to the room opens from outside. There is a moment where no one appears, the person that opened the door hesitating before crossing the threshold.

GERRY: Paul?

No answer.

Len?

Now GERRY sees him.

Len.

LEN, in a full-length raincoat, enters.

Beneath the coat LEN is in a bespoke suit. His shirt has French cuffs, fastened with tasteful, perhaps jewelled, cufflinks. LEN looks around, and through the audience.

LEN: There's nobody here.

GERRY: Paul had to go get Danny.

LEN: Get Danny where?

GERRY: A place.

LEN: A place downtown?

GERRY: Yeah, downtown, I guess. Wherever, you know.

LEN: Don't actually.

Beat.

But can guess.

GERRY: Paul had an idea where to find him.

LEN: Paul had an idea?

Beat.

Danny is… Danny's always been the one I worried about.

GERRY: But it wasn't Danny, was it?

LEN: No.

Beat.

What is this place?

GERRY: A few years ago Paul started his own business. After he and Virginia came back from California. It was, like, custom…

GERRY tries to remember what it was that PAUL was planning but can't recall. He looks at the machinery to jog his memory but it is no help.

High-end custom…

He can't make himself remember what it was.

…you know?

LEN looks about.

LEN: Can see it's thriving.

GERRY: Now he…

LEN: …works as a hostess for his father-in-law.

LEN nods at GERRY as if to say, "Yes, that is true."

I've done business with Arthur Whalen.

Beat.

Ginnie, Virginia, was actually in a couple of movies, hey? When they went out to Los Angeles she...

GERRY: So I understood. I've never seen...

LEN: Better actress than you'd think. She was in *The Nevada Girl* and, what was it called?

(remembers) Total Conquest.

GERRY: That's right, you and Virginia... before she and Paul...

LEN cuts him off.

LEN: How long has Lionel been in custody?

GERRY takes off his windbreaker and puts it over the back of a chair.

GERRY: Early this morning.

LEN: Early?

GERRY: Four in the morning.

This information shocks LEN.

This is second-hand. Paul heard something at a business lunch. Pounding on the door, middle of the night, warrants.

LEN: Jesus.

GERRY: Element of surprise. They want you disoriented I guess.

LEN: No opportunity to destroy evidence.

GERRY: I hadn't thought of that.

LEN checks his watch.

LEN: Four in the morning... still in custody?

GERRY: I was going to check again. When the guys were here, I'd go check.

LEN: How do you do that?

GERRY: I drive past his house. See if his car's back. Debbie, that's his wife...

LEN: *(impatiently)* I've met Debbie.

GERRY: I presume she's down there at the cop shop with him.

LEN: Or getting a lawyer.

GERRY: Yeah, I guess.

LEN: She hasn't gone out for chicken.

GERRY: No.

LEN: So you drive past?

GERRY: So, yeah… their cars. I drive past once, see if they're back.

LEN: I guess that's the best you can do.

GERRY: Can't phone.

LEN: No, absolutely not. Can't even answer.

GERRY: Bail?

LEN: Unless he's a flight risk.

Long beat.

GERRY: Is he?

LEN: I don't know.

Beat.

GERRY: Are you?

LEN thinks about it.

LEN: I have a lot here.

GERRY: Are you?

LEN snaps at GERRY.

LEN: Of course. Yes. You would have to be. You would have to consider that possibility.

Beat.

"A flight risk." Always "a risk" of something, uncertainty. Could just as well say "a possibility."

GERRY: Don't confuse it with "an opportunity."

LEN: I don't know… am I "a flight opportunity"…? maybe.

Beat.

I'd played it all out, all the possible scenarios. Most of them with Danny fucking up to start it.

GERRY: For me. Lots.

LEN: Movies of it playing in your head at night? *The Too Late Show?*

GERRY: *(answering)* Unfocused panic. Sitting at my desk, talking with a student, giving a lecture. I worried about the consequences, the ultimate…

LEN: That's why we're here.

Beat.

Can't phone.

GERRY: No. Because we don't know what they know… or… when Lionel…

LEN: When Lionel will…?

GERRY: He will confess. Nobody expects heroics.

LEN: Nobody.

GERRY: Men talk tough…

LEN: Yeah, mostly that's all. And Lionel… he's…

GERRY: *(simultaneously)* …weak.

LEN: *(simultaneously)* …brave.

Beat.

Do we know…

LEN becomes grave.

Do we know if it's directly linked to… Why, at this moment, did they grab Lionel?

GERRY: Paul will know.

LEN: How?

GERRY: He just said.

LEN: He knows where to find Danny; he knows what's up with Lionel.

GERRY: He says. He's stayed in contact.

LEN: Not with me.

GERRY: With me. With Danny to some degree, obviously.

LEN: I've seen Paul a few times, business functions, across a room, nod at each other, but he's never come over to say hello.

GERRY: Have you ever gone over to say…?

LEN: No. I deal with Whalen and other "people" from the outfit; I've taken meetings over there, but I've never had reason to see Paul.

GERRY: What, so you think he was avoiding you?

LEN scoffs.

LEN: No! Nothing like that. Just that he doesn't… attend those meetings, *you know.*

GERRY doesn't know.

I haven't seen you in…?

GERRY: No, long time, hey. Was it at the liquor store there… five or six…?

LEN: No. I don't think so.

GERRY: I was away for a few years. I did my graduate work out… and then a couple of teaching jobs… until the position came up here.

LEN: Returned to the scene of the crime.

GERRY: No. Well, obviously, yes… but…

LEN: Irresistible urge to do that. To go back to the place where the deed was done.

GERRY: That's not the case with me.

LEN: Sure.

GERRY: Really.

LEN: I believe you. I've had no urge, nothing to resist.

GERRY: Don't dwell in the past?

LEN: Tried not to have one, holds you back.

Beat. LEN snaps his fingers and points at GERRY.

Wait, you're right. I do remember. It was… the liquor store on…

GERRY: Yeah, on… you know…

LEN: Yeah. That was a busy time for me. Good busy. How have things been for you?

GERRY: It's complicated.

LEN: Like us all.

GERRY: More so in my case, I think.

LEN raises his eyebrows.

It's not something that I particularly want to… Hey, my problems *are* more complicated than yours, okay.

LEN: You don't know my problems.

GERRY: Are they your kid's problems?

That's a bomb.

LEN: No. No. Nothing like that. Of course.

GERRY: Sorry. Your problems?

LEN: None of much substance until now.

Beat.

Do you suppose…?

GERRY: Do I suppose what?

LEN: Nothing. Forget it.

LEN marches away.

GERRY: Bet I know.

LEN says nothing.

Do I suppose it's just a scare, a false alarm? Something else altogether?

LEN takes off his raglan raincoat. He nods yes.

That's the thought I'm holding on to. I'm polishing it.

LEN: That's what it is… it's something else. It's a scare. We don't have the facts. You watch, it's just a scare.

LEN looks for a clean place to put his raincoat but finally gives up, throwing it carelessly on a dusty bench.

Silence. LEN walks to a window and looks out. He turns back and faces GERRY.

I didn't even know you had a kid.

GERRY: He's four. He's got deficits, okay.

LEN: Jesus that is… that is very rough. I'm sorry. Now with this.

GERRY: I know.

Long beat.

LEN: I remember, back when we said what we would do. What we would do in the event of… I know it's ridiculous now. We talked about a plan. You said. You said you would run.

GERRY: I thought that at the time. I was, like, twenty-one, what did I know?

LEN: Your kid's problems, they're like…?

GERRY: Let's just say I shouldn't even be here.

Beat.

You have three, right?

LEN: Three?

GERRY: Children.

LEN doesn't seem pleased by the thought.

LEN: Yes. Three. Youngest is eight years old, John.

GERRY: You and Lynn already had the first girl…

GERRY has forgotten the name.

LEN: Jackie, yeah. That was a surprise.

Beat.

I saw Danny a few years ago.

GERRY: Yeah?

LEN: Yeah. I was downtown, Christmas shopping WITH MY KIDS. And I come out of this store, you know the place, Samara.

GERRY: Know of it. Not really… my range.

LEN: He's standing there, Danny, waiting for me. Probably saw me through the window. He's, you know, stinking of something. It's booze but also… paint thinner or glue. Solvents. His face was all cut up.

LEN gestures, waving an invisible knife or spike at GERRY's face.

There's snot hanging out of his nose. He says, get this, he says "Merry Christmas." And then... he starts to go "Ho Ho Ho" but takes a coughing fit. He goes—

LEN hacks it out.

"Houghht Houghht Houghhhhhht." I'm with my kids. He's hacking away, this snot on his nose is swinging back and forth. Then I notice... Then I notice that he's shit himself. He's got shit in his pants.

GERRY: What did you say to him?

LEN: What can you say? Nothing. I pretended like I didn't even know him. I move the kids along.

GERRY: He's gone to a bad place.

LEN: Christmas. I was with my kids.

GERRY: I understand.

There is a silence. The true gravity of the situation is beginning to hit LEN.

LEN: GODDAMN FUCKING LIONEL! We can't let this happen.

GERRY: How are we going to...

LEN: We figure it out. I have got too much to lose.

GERRY: All of us.

LEN: Except Danny.

GERRY: No.

LEN: Prison might be the best thing for him. Maybe he'd get help.

GERRY: Help he hasn't asked for.

LEN: He doesn't even... we could...

GERRY: What?

LEN: Make it worth his while.

GERRY: To go to prison?

LEN: He's in one already.

GERRY: That's good, that's very good—you're some advocate for street people now. "He's in one already." That's too good.

LEN: I'm thinking of options.

GERRY: What? Say the thing was Danny's idea?

LEN: No, obviously not him… but he had to be involved, to open the doors, so he's done anyway. They'll know he was working there then. *The security guard?* Always one of the first suspects, pal.

GERRY: Inside job.

LEN: Always are.

GERRY snaps back into focus.

GERRY: We let Danny and Lionel take the blame?

LEN: We compensate them.

GERRY: Jesus.

LEN: Gerry, that's how things really happen. Even the prosecutors cut deals… everything's business; you negotiate everything.

GERRY: Compensate them?

LEN: Financially.

GERRY: That is not going to happen. Even if, I'm not in a position to…

LEN: What's not going to happen is me going to prison. I have the dough. Paul can get Ginnie to write a cheque, it'll be grocery money for her.

GERRY: I think… I was going to wait till we were all here to put this forward, but I think we approach, through a lawyer—we approach the university and offer to pay the money back.

LEN: Now that they're on to you? Now that you're caught? And do you think offering to pay it back now, almost ten years later is…

GERRY: Almost twenty years…

LEN: No.

GERRY: Yeah.

This news hits LEN as hard as anything. He pulls out a chair and, without bothering to brush off the abundant dust, sits on it.

LEN: Right you are. Jackie will be eighteen… next month.

GERRY: What's the equivalent in, like, today's money?

LEN: How much did we steal?

GERRY: Steal? I…

LEN: It was, what, $160,000 back then, now that's about $250,000. Compound interest…

LEN puts his head back and thinks it through.

Half million bucks.

GERRY: Bullshit!

LEN: That's what it is. At a shitty rate.

GERRY: No, it can't…

GERRY loses his breath.

LEN: That's what I do, Gerry. I work the numbers. It's true. It's the miracle of compound interest. Didn't you read *The Wealthy Barber*?

GERRY: No… I got my RRSPs with the university. We used to. We cashed them in, like…

LEN anticipates GERRY's next line and silently mouths "At the bottom of the market."

…at exactly the worst time… but there was work on the house that had to be done, and… there were some medical expenses… just some bad decisions. I've never been good with… Really? That much? Sometimes… well, I think it was like a prank.

LEN shakes his head no.

LEN: It's serious theft. Front-page-picture-of-you-dragged-from-the-courtroom-in-shackles-weeping kind of stealing.

Beat.

If we're lucky it'll come out on a day when there is bad news, some massive disaster, some towelheads-flying-planes-into-the-building type catastrophe. Then we might get blown to page three or four. Then people won't look away, won't pretend you're not there. Instead they'll come up to you at the mall or the supermarket and say "Gerry, wasn't there something about you in the paper? Your kid won something at the Kiwanis Music Festival, was it?" And you can say, "Oh thaaat, a minor larceny thing, back when I was in university, a little theft over five thousand *prank.* How have you been, Ron, commit any crimes yourself? Do any good-natured thieving like you're old buddy Gerry?"

Beat.

There are pricks I do business with, people like Whalen and Frank Stafford, that whole crowd, who are going to see it as confirmation of something they have long believed: That I didn't come from the right sort of background. That I would take it with my bare hands instead of with a knife and fork.

LEN *changes gears.*

It's serious theft. It's enough money to have us put away, and you know what, at the very same time, it's so little money as to be embarrassing.

LEN *needs to takes a breath.*

Real players, men I've met, with whom I have done business… it's millions of dollars.

LEN *shakes his head.*

Welcome to the small time, Gerry. We're going to take it hard. For grand theft that's petty.

GERRY: You'll have to come down much further than the rest of us.

LEN: Fucking right.

GERRY: A professor of little distinction, I couldn't understand that.

LEN: Did I already say "fuck you, Gerry."

GERRY: We all have a lot to lose.

LEN: Yeah, I guess this is one of a few things that can get you sacked at the academy, hey?

GERRY: *(sardonicly)* I'm tenured so, "Fuck you too, Len."

Beat.

It seemed like a lark.

LEN: Even when you were spending the money?

GERRY: More so then.

LEN: I didn't spend it; I invested it; I had a kid coming; I did something with it.

GERRY: Well good for you. You are a paragon of capitalism.

LEN: I HAVEN'T TAKEN MY FUN YET!

GERRY: That's nothing to do with the money. That's you, that's the way you chose to live your life.

LEN: I made responsible decisions.

GERRY: With stolen money.

Beat.

LEN: So the mom?

It takes GERRY a second to follow the change in subject.

GERRY: Of our child? Brian is the boy's name. Mom is Sheila Winters. Great woman. Just the best.

LEN: How long have you guys been...?

GERRY: I don't know, nine years; she's not from here.

LEN: No?

GERRY: I was teaching...

GERRY gestures westward.

...and I met her there.

LEN: Grad student?

GERRY: So fucking what.

LEN: So fucking nothing. So fucking relax.

Beat.

She?

GERRY: What?

LEN: Did you ever... tell her?

Beat.

GERRY: I thought I should.

LEN stops breathing over a long beat. GERRY and LEN stare at one another. Their eyes have truly met and locked for the first time this evening.

But no.

LEN resumes breathing.

LEN: Sure?

GERRY: Yeah, sure. You ever?

LEN: Say anything? No. That would just bring them into it, implicate them.

GERRY: Exactly, that's exactly what I thought. It won't go over great. She's gonna say I didn't trust her but...

LEN: No, that's not the case. With your wife. It's different.

GERRY: It's to spare her the attendant anxiety.

Now it is impossible to tell whether LEN is being sarcastic or genuine or... and there is no word for it... both at once.

LEN: You're magnanimous, Ger, big-hearted.

GERRY: She's not going to see it that way.

LEN: Don't think she'll "be there" for you?

GERRY: I... sure she will.

LEN: Because it turns out you're not the man she thought she married.

GERRY: She...

LEN: And it's important for the jury, you know, to see the family standing behind you.

GERRY: Nobody can know... entirely know, any person. You don't make a pact to reveal everything.

LEN: No?

GERRY: No. And one act, a long time ago...

LEN: We are what we do. What we've done. We are our actions.

GERRY: That's not entirely true. That's not the whole story.

LEN: Yeah, it is. I suppose you are... what? Your intentions? Hey? Your actions: not only did you take the money, you kept that secret to yourself. Kept it from lovely Sheila. Now, hearing the hounds on the piss scent of your fear, you've decided you're going to confess.

GERRY: You think Lynn will "be there" for you?

LEN has to think about it.

LEN: There was a time she would have been... she always was... but I think she finally saw that I was embarrassed by that, by being helped along. And I wonder sometimes if she mistook that for my being ashamed of her. I should know better what she thinks but I... I've stopped asking.

LEN shakes off the thought.

But for the public humiliation she'd probably just as soon see the back of me.

GERRY: The humiliation is a big part of it, I guess.

LEN laughs at GERRY.

LEN: Yeah, Ger. That's the biggest part of it. That's what it is.

Stealthily DANNY has entered, coming up from behind the other two, without LEN knowing. DANNY has tried to keep himself together but his clothes, clearly freebies from the back door of some church, are dirty. His hair is dirty. He is thin and drawn. He's toothless or possibly wearing ill-fitting dentures. He is ghostly.

The whole village gathers round for your comeuppance, to see you brought down.

DANNY: That's justice.

LEN jumps with surprise.

LEN: Jesus!

DANNY: Be calm.

LEN: You startled me.

DANNY: Paul told me to, you know, be smooth. Try not to draw attention to myself. I can do it. I'm like a-a rabbit... or... a, whaddaya call? A hare! You know, coat changing in the weather, white against the snow.

GERRY: Hello, Danny.

Did DANNY hear him?

DANNY: I can be downtown, in the steam and the yelling, and be invisible. You don't have to worry about me. I'm gone.

LEN: Where is Paul?

DANNY: He's parking the car away from the…

DANNY looks around, sizing the place up.

…parking the car away from the building.

GERRY: I guess that's prudent.

DANNY: Paul is like… freaking. He's been watching a lot of cop shows on TV or something. He's excited. Thinks he's Mannix. Paul's pumped.

LEN: "Pumped"? We're all "pumped," Danny, because we're in shit.

DANNY shrugs.

DANNY: Maybe. Guess I'm used to shit. I have habituated shit. I'm not that excited. Paul should take something… for the excitement.

DANNY takes a seat.

GERRY: *(to DANNY)* Paul explained what's happening?

DANNY: To Lionel, now, tonight?

LEN: Yeah.

DANNY nods.

GERRY: Good.

DANNY: But… what? To tell you the truth. The truth, right. I was never, maybe I was once but… I had some forgetting, okay… but I'm fuzzy on…

DANNY drifts off for a moment, not finishing.

LEN: …on?

DANNY: I never understand how the deed was done. Hey, don't get me wrong, I took my cut, I'm not… you know… I'm in with everybody, I'm not, you know, number one, lookin' out for… but… but…

Beat.

I didn't know what the fuck was goin' on.

LEN: In general?

DANNY: Not…

DANNY makes an expansive waving gesture of his arms.

…not, like, totally in general, like universal, no. I meant, yeah, you could say "in general in terms of the job." But like in general, "in general" I sooooo know what's goin' on.

DANNY points at LEN.

Probably more than you.

DANNY begins to light a cigarette.

GERRY: Ah… do… Danny? Do you have to smoke in here?

DANNY doesn't stop.

DANNY: Yes.

DANNY takes a deep drag. LEN looks on longingly.

So.

LEN: "So," what?

DANNY: What exactly did you guys do that we now deserve our "comeuppance."

LEN: Danny?

DANNY: Yeah?

LEN: Do you have another cigarette?

Now DANNY stands and walks towards LEN. DANNY affects a tremor and extends a shaking hand, clutching a pack of smokes, offering one to LEN, but as if he were begging.

DANNY: Got a spare smoke, man?

LEN uncomfortably takes a cigarette and a lighter from DANNY.

You fall upon hard times, Len?

LEN: No.

DANNY: That you can't afford a deck of smokes?

LEN: No, I quit.

DANNY: Right, I can see that.

DANNY returns to his seat. LEN lights his cigarette and relishes the smoke.

So?

LEN: The broad strokes are…

GERRY: They were changing the operating system of the computers at University Administration, UNIX to Linux. Operating systems are…

DANNY: Addict, not retard.

GERRY: We, or rather Lionel, saw there would be a gap, "an opportunity" in the way the computer accounted for…

LEN has no patience for this pained and detailed explanation.

LEN: Money was moved out of the registrar and the bookstore and… a couple of other places.

GERRY: Len did the tombstoning…

LEN flinches at this description.

…opened bank accounts in the names of dead people.

LEN: Withdrew it from ATMs over a couple of weeks. Hundred and sixty thousand dollars, thirty grand each.

Beat.

DANNY: "Moved"? The money was "moved"?

LEN: Well…

DANNY: Forgive me, of the "movers and the shakers"… I'm with the shakers, so "moving"… Wait, why did you need me to…?

GERRY: User names and passwords…

LEN: …from the personal computers of some people in the university administration.

DANNY: Just stealing the passwords?

LEN: Paul said two of them were written on yellow stickies attached to the monitors.

GERRY: "Ulysses."

LEN: "Charlie123."

GERRY: And the dean of arts was the…

LEN & GERRY: "Pussymeister."

GERRY: *(to DANNY)* That's why we needed you to let Paul into their offices, to… "recover" the passwords.

DANNY: Paul asked me. I would have done anything for him.

DANNY looks back to the door for PAUL.

LEN: Where is Paul? Where did he park the...

DANNY interrupts.

DANNY: Wait... one hundred and sixty thousand... then...

LEN: Lionel got the extra ten because... he figured out how to do it.

DANNY: Lionel was one of the original computer geeks, hey?

GERRY: That's sort of true.

DANNY: Some of those guys, they made money, they wrote the new rules. They made it their world, right? Bill Gates and all that.

GERRY: Some of them.

LEN: Most of them ended up with crap systems jobs and never learned how to talk to girls.

DANNY: I was hoping there was more to it. The way you guys let on... It's always like that, crime, real crime, up close, it's always... embarrassing.

LEN: Sorry to disappoint a man of such discerning standards.

DANNY: Paul asked me. Paul, not you.

Beat.

And I read all the books, you know.

GERRY: What books?

DANNY: The books you guys had to read for your courses. Most of them. Not textbooks but, like, literature and history and stuff. The real books. I'd see you with them at the science caf and then if the same book showed up in the lost and found, or if I found one left behind during a night shift, I'd read it. No biggie. I read the books.

LEN: I didn't.

GERRY: What?

LEN: I didn't read the books. That's the trick, Danny. They give you the degree because you can pretend you read the books.

DANNY: Pretend?

GERRY: Bullshit.

LEN laughs.

LEN: No. It's true. Got me through law school. Nothing wrong with reading the books, Danny. I mean it's great, but it's got nothing to do with... you know. And look at poor Gerry here; he read those books and he still remembers them. He cannot get them out of his mind. Can you imagine that?

DANNY: I remember that money. What did you guys do with it?

DANNY laughs.

Pay off your student loans?

GERRY: I...

LEN cuts him off.

LEN: I didn't have loans. Worked weekends and summers at Empire Packers. Poultry.

GERRY: I... I guess... I didn't like squander it but... it was gone very quickly.

GERRY is struck by a thought, puts his hand to his head. He disengages from LEN and DANNY and walks away. It's as though he is trying to remember something.

DANNY: My cut?

DANNY laughs.

Partied.

LEN: Put it up your nose?

DANNY: Sure, sometimes. Or in my arm. Straight in my blood or drank it. Set it afire, huffed the fumes. Whaddaya got? Whaddaya have on ya? I'll take it! I can't resist life's rich bounty.

LEN: Jesus.

LEN and DANNY's talk is too much for GERRY. It's interfering with his thinking.

GERRY: *(to no one in particular)* Shush!

DANNY: Come off it, I'm telling the truth... besides, there soon won't be anything to hide.

LEN: Is that what Paul told you?

DANNY: He said they arrested Lionel, that Lionel would talk and so we were caught, that the law was coming. And Len... what is that, "Len"?

LEN: What's what?

DANNY: The name. Is that like short for "Lenneth"?

LEN: "Lenneth"? No, Leonard.

DANNY: Whaddaya got, Lenneth? Got anything on ya? What's the pain-management situation?

LEN: Me? No. I have nothing on me.

DANNY: (to GERRY) Lenneth and I grew up on the same street, you know that, Gerry?

GERRY *isn't listening.*

Little snot-nosed Lenny. "Here, Lenny, go get me five smokes and buy yourself a fucking Pixy Stix for the trouble."

GERRY: I can't...

LEN: You can't "what"?

GERRY: I can't account for my cut. I frittered it away. Did I? I bought a second-hand Datsun. I took that trip to Germany. I paid the rent... I... I spent it like it was money.

LEN: What else would it be like?

GERRY: Now, money... it's everything. I never stop thinking about it, worrying, calculating. My pension. The cost of this versus that. The mortgage. The car payments. The Visa bill. I get up in the morning and I'm thinking of money, how I can't quit my job because I need the money, paying money, not having enough money. Money's not money anymore... it's the medium in which I exist.

PAUL *enters. He is wearing smart, casual clothes, crisp and clean, with no wear. He wears glasses with fashionable, though conservative, designer frames. He looks very much as if a woman dressed him. He has a confidence in carriage and speech that has been learned. He speaks crisply.*

DANNY: (to PAUL) Hi, Paul.

LEN: (to PAUL) How did you find out about Lionel?

PAUL *doesn't even seem to hear* DANNY. *He responds to* LEN.

PAUL: Lunch meeting at Brasserie St. Pierre, Markus Wellfoort…

LEN *nods. He knows this Markus Wellfoort.*

…told Arthur. Markus lives just down the street from Lionel, seemed to know him a bit, kids in soccer. Markus was going for a jog. Apparently the people at Lionel's were distraught.

LEN: Going for a jog at four in the morning?

PAUL: I didn't say it was four in the morning.

GERRY: Sure you did.

PAUL: No. Early. I said early in the morning.

LEN: What time did Markus say it was?

PAUL: He didn't. He was going for a run or coming back from one.

LEN: That makes a big difference, Paul. He's coming back from a run… it could be closer to eight in the morning. Maybe it was near a shift change for the cops, then it's different than if they meant to catch him off his guard. It makes all the difference.

PAUL: I didn't see how it could be important. I was thinking of the larger picture.

LEN: See, Paul, this is why you're…

LEN *won't finish the thought out loud. Another thought occurs to him.*

At this lunch with Markus Wellfoort, you didn't let on that you knew Lionel?

PAUL: No.

LEN: Did they know any details, why he'd been arrested?

PAUL *shakes his head.*

PAUL: Arthur said that Lionel had approached us a year or so ago. Lionel wanted us to partner on something, take an equity position.

GERRY: Like what?

PAUL: I don't know any more than we took a pass. On that particular file I wasn't part of the discussion.

LEN: *(to* GERRY*)* Not part of the discussion.

(back to PAUL) So why do we think this business with the cops at Lionel's has anything to do with us?

PAUL: Arthur seemed to know, and Markus too, that there were problems with Lionel's financial statements. Irregularities. Things didn't add up over there.

LEN *nods. He seems to know what this means.*

GERRY: So? Lionel's got problems now. Nothing to do with us.

PAUL: If there's a forensic audit.

GERRY: They won't go back that far. Will they?

LEN: If there's one thing that smells and they decide to dig…

PAUL: They look at his bank statements, see a series of large cash deposits made back in the day…

LEN: And then there's the question of whether Lionel might want to cut a deal.

The others look as though they need an elaboration.

They have him on this thing now, he says to the cops, "Do you think you guys could cut me some slack if I told about this other thing. It's a great story, I think you know how it begins."

PAUL: And Lionel tells them what happened next.

GERRY: And this is how it ends.

PAUL *surveys the room, checking the lights. He is unhappy with what he sees. He goes first to the interior shutters and closes them.*

PAUL: You guys shouldn't have parked out front.

GERRY: You're right. Wasn't thinking.

LEN: Why not?

PAUL: Why not, what?

LEN: Park out front.

PAUL: If they're looking for us they'll have our licence-plate numbers.

GERRY: *(to himself)* Looking for us?

LEN: And, otherwise? We're going to get away on foot? Call a taxi?

PAUL: We haven't decided what to do yet.

PAUL now turns on the available lamps, the utility bulbs in their cages and the lamp above the covered table. He then turns off the overhead light. The dialogue continues as he does so.

LEN: "We"?

PAUL: Besides, "getting away"? It's a ridiculous idea.

GERRY: As Len reminds me… that was the plan.

PAUL: Plans change with the circumstances.

LEN: The circumstances haven't changed, the circumstances have arisen. We are in, and of, and all over the circumstances.

PAUL: *(condescendingly)* Fantasy! That talk, running, we were young.

LEN: You're as young as you feel.

DANNY: Or as old as last night.

LEN: What are the alternatives?

PAUL: *(scoffs)* You would really try to run? Where to?

(to GERRY and DANNY) Len on the lam!

LEN: I haven't ruled out any options. What are yours?

PAUL: I think it's obvious we get a lawyer to go to the police and begin some sort of negotiations.

LEN blows.

LEN: GODDAMMIT!

GERRY: We've been through all that.

LEN: It's too late, Paul.

GERRY: He's right, there's… we have nothing to offer. Len thinks we could cut…

GERRY realizes that LEN had included DANNY in this formulation.

…Lionel loose.

PAUL: What?

GERRY: For a fee.

PAUL: A fee? To go to prison for us? Die for our sins?

GERRY: Would his sentence be that much worse?

LEN: And he'd have something waiting for him on the other side. The way it goes down now, he does the time and he gets out and he's ruined anyway.

GERRY: We. We are ruined.

DANNY: You. You are ruined. I have nothing. The cops are going to ask Lionel how he got the passwords, who helped him. First thing the police always ask, "Where did your friends go?" They'll check some records, my name will be on the list. I was the security guard for fuck's sake...

GERRY: *(whispering/mouthing to himself)* Inside job.

DANNY: ...I mean, that's always the first suspect.

LEN: "Your friends"?

DANNY: In the sense of co-conspirators.

DANNY now screams like a bad cop squeezing a suspect.

"**WHERE DID YOUR FUCKING FRIENDS GO!**"

They are all quiet for a moment.

GERRY: That's a funny way to think of friendship.

DANNY: That's part of it, that's something a true friend will do for you. Friends provide an alibi.

PAUL: You mean "accomplice," not "friend."

DANNY: What's the diff?

GERRY: Loyalty?

PAUL: Stop it. We aren't cutting Lionel or anybody loose.

LEN: Paul, do me a favour and speak for yourself, okay. Get off this den mother thing. You're not in charge.

PAUL: No? Are you?

LEN: No. I'm looking out for myself.

PAUL: Now, when it's convenient.

LEN: What's that supposed to mean?

PAUL: You got us into this mess.

LEN is staggered.

LEN: Me?

PAUL: You're the one that made us do it.

LEN: It was Lionel's idea.

PAUL: It was just an idea, it was just talk.

LEN: Give me a break.

PAUL: It was. I remember. It was in the science caf. Lionel was talking about it the day before. You wouldn't let it go. Lionel had this idea and you were the one that pushed it.

LEN: I pressured you?

PAUL: Something like that.

LEN: Because I had the guts to go through with it? I made you take the money?

PAUL: You bullied us.

LEN: "Bullied"? Jesus, this is too much.

(to GERRY) Did I bully you, Gerry? Danny?

GERRY can't meet LEN's gaze. Neither GERRY or DANNY can answer.

No.

GERRY: You said yourself you were in a desperate situation; you had a kid on the way.

LEN points at PAUL.

LEN: You "recovered" the passwords.

LEN turns to GERRY.

And you were the one that told Lionel they were going to switch the systems.

GERRY: Maybe "bullied" isn't the… If it hadn't been for you, we wouldn't have gone through with it.

LEN: You guys had your own reasons. Paul didn't even need the money.

GERRY: That said, I did it. We did it. We took the money. And… I mean I was scared but… I was excited too. I haven't been so excited.

DANNY: I didn't feel any pressure. It started rolling and I went with it. Maybe Len gave me a push. But I need a push.

DANNY laughs.

I'm not a self-starter.

Beat.

Mostly I did it because Paul asked me to.

This is a small victory for LEN.

LEN: Ohhhh! Did he coerce you, Danny? Did Paul bend your pincushion of an arm?

DANNY: No. I would have done anything for Paul because I was in love with him.

LEN: Love? LOVE?

PAUL is embarrassed, confused, and angry.

PAUL: Fuck off, Danny.

DANNY: It's true.

PAUL: Listen...

LEN: "In love." I think that is just so adorable.

GERRY: *(to LEN)* Stop it.

LEN: Maybe it wasn't me after all, maybe it was all for love.

DANNY: I don't want to make you uncomfortable, Paul. But it's true. I don't know how sexual...

PAUL: Please, Danny.

DANNY: You know I'm not like... totally gay or anything. Back when I was partying a lot I had sex with men...

LEN: Yippee! This is good.

PAUL: Stop it, Danny.

DANNY: ...women, it didn't matter, it was full-time happiness of all kinds, you know.

(to PAUL) But with you it was different.

LEN: Not "totally" gay? You get that, Paul?

GERRY: Stop it, Len.

DANNY: I mean I'm not part of that scene. Homosexual. Heterosexual. Both sound kinda gross when you say them. I think I might have been the original metrosexual, you know. I would basically fuck the entire city.

GERRY: I think "metrosexual" means...

LEN points at PAUL behind PAUL's back.

DANNY: I know what it means. Joke. Now, like for a few years, basically after I lost my teeth in this beating I took... now I'm like... nothing... sexually. It's not part of my life anymore. These social-services dentures, they don't even fit.

Beat.

A lot of my self-esteem was in those pearly whites. No matter what sort of situation, no matter where I'd gotten myself to, I always took care of them. I'm pretty sure my mom got that into my head, that I should brush them three times a day. And I did. There were a few times there when the only thing I owned was a toothbrush.

Beat.

She maybe, my mom, she maybe should have given me more detailed instructions.

DANNY seems to have run out of gas. Something comes to him.

You want to know my fantasy?

PAUL: Not really.

LEN: YES!

DANNY: I'd like to be a stay-at-home mom.

LEN and PAUL and GERRY have nothing to say.

Making lunches and pots of soup and mac and cheese, and stuffing loot bags. Busy, you know, around the house, cleaning and ironing. Putting the kids to bed. It seems to me that's how I'd be most happy.

The other men are still speechless.

Hey, look, I know it's a fantasy. I know at this point in my life that the stay-at-home mom thing is not a realistic option.

Beat.

Definitely not gonna happen if we do time.

LEN: When I grow up I'm going play centre for the Habs. Any of you guys want a dumb-tit to help you through this?

PAUL: My therapist says those sorts of fantasies, thoughts of another life, they're natural.

Beat.

LEN: Therapist?

PAUL: Yes. What about it?

LEN: Nothing.

(quickly) You didn't tell him?

PAUL: Her.

LEN: Then "her."

PAUL: About this?

PAUL gestures around.

No.

LEN: Why were you seeing a therapist?

PAUL: *Am* seeing, and it's none of your business.

LEN: But nothing to do with this...

LEN, perfectly mimicking PAUL, gestures to the room they are in.

...or matters arising, like Danny's undying love for you?

PAUL: LISTEN! This is the first I've heard of that, okay. I tried to help Danny on a couple of occasions but I didn't ask for that.

This obviously hurts DANNY and he flinches.

(to DANNY) I'm sorry but that's the truth. I don't even know where you're coming from with that shit.

DANNY: *(sheepishly)* I'm fine.

He's not.

LEN: *(to PAUL)* You're sure you told this head-shrinker nothing about...

PAUL: I see her for depression, okay. I was depressed.

LEN: And...?

PAUL: Oh, fuck you. It's an illness.

GERRY: It is.

DANNY: Definitely.

LEN: I don't doubt it. And you self-medicated with alcohol, right? What a shocker. Life is short, then you die, usually badly, in the end it's meaningless and along the way shit like this...

LEN *gestures to the room they are in.*

...happens to you.

LEN *makes two fists and smashes them together.*

Self-awareness and mortality? Jesus, you're supposed to be depressed. In the face of it what else are you gonna do, throw a party?

Beat.

DANNY: Well... obviously... yeah.

GERRY *applauds.*

GERRY: Sometimes, Danny...

LEN: You got it, Danny, get over yourself and put your cock in.

DANNY: When I was in the joint they made me do therapy.

That DANNY has been in "the joint" is news to LEN and GERRY. PAUL knew.

GERRY: "The joint"?

DANNY: Means penitentiary.

GERRY: Yes.

DANNY: The psychiatrist there, she said that everybody inside, all the other inmates, every one of them was a narcissist. That was why they could commit crimes.

LEN: When were you in prison?

DANNY: I'm a lot of things. A... lot... of... things. But I am not a narcissist. Guess they don't have a "junkie fuck-up" box to tick. They should though, because, like, in the penal system it is not an uncommon...

LEN: WHEN WERE YOU IN?

DANNY: Incarcerated? Went in, or got out?

LEN: Both.

DANNY: It wasn't like… you know… federal time or anything. Just ten months, and that's only because I had a previous… narcotics… offence.

Beat.

I broke into this house. The prosecutor tried to sell it as like "a home invasion" but…

Beat.

I didn't know the people were there! The car was gone. Turns out they'd left it at a restaurant and taken a cab because they'd had a couple of glasses of wine. Can you believe that? Wow. That is some kind of discipline, to do that. Not to take the car after a couple of glasses of wine… with dinner. Even… goin' out to dinner and having wine. A house. Job, I guess, to do that. Friends that won't cheat ya. What do they have for dinner at those places? Like duck and steaks, I guess…

He snaps out of a reverie.

I pled out. That was five or six years ago.

Beat.

If I'd told that head doctor about us you would have known by now. I served four months.

Long beat.

Good behaviour!

DANNY finds this absolutely hilarious. He cracks up laughing until he is stopped by a fit of coughing.

It was in all the papers… but the back pages. Small-time.

GERRY: How was it?

DANNY: How was prison? Very bad. Punishing, yeah. I think that's on purpose. No duck on the menu.

When they put me away this time… given my record… it'll be federal.

DANNY turns to PAUL.

If you didn't tell your *therapist* about the robbery…

GERRY winces hearing the word. He thrusts his hands out as if to stop it coming.

GERRY: Don't say "robbery." Please.

DANNY: …then you were wasting your time.

PAUL: I don't think…

DANNY: Sure you were. I mean this has weighed on your mind and you didn't mention it.

PAUL: It hasn't weighed on my mind. I've gotten along just fine.

GERRY: Bullshit. This is… it's an unresolved issue.

LEN: *(to himself)* I can't believe this.

PAUL: I see my therapist for a different life, a life that has nothing to do with what we have done. I see her about the life I have that I want, not the goddamn past.

GERRY: You can't have different lives. You have one life.

PAUL: No. Wrong. We are all different people at different times. We change to… deal… with what we have to deal with.

DANNY: Gotta know your alias.

PAUL: The only people that know the people in this room, that know the people that… did that… are the other three.

LEN: You want to know why I think people go to therapy?

PAUL: Not particularly.

LEN makes a masturbatory action with his hand.

LEN: To get stroked.

PAUL nods sarcastically, yeah, yeah here it comes, he's heard it before…

To have someone pay attention. You want someone to pretend to be interested in your self-pitying bullshit, to pretend to care? You gotta pay a therapist? Why not get a whore and have a fuck too on the same ticket? It's all wankery.

DANNY: It cost a lot to get a whore to pretend to care.

GERRY: *(to PAUL)* If you're keeping stuff from the therapist…

PAUL: It's not a cure, okay?

Something occurs to LEN.

LEN: *(to* PAUL*)* Never said anything to Ginnie?

PAUL: No.

LEN: To anyone?

PAUL *avoids* LEN's *gaze.*

Paul, you haven't told anyone?

PAUL: Not… I didn't in any specific terms.

LEN: Who did you tell?

PAUL: A girl. A girlfriend. An out-of-town girlfriend.

This is met with a deadly silence.

She'd never say anything.

Long silence.

LEN: Young?

PAUL: Younger.

LEN: She impressed? The wife dresses you but, underneath, you're really a tough guy.

PAUL: Enough. She won't say anything.

LEN: "Don't park the cars out front."

LEN *turns from* PAUL *and walks away shaking his head. It's a feint for after a couple of steps he spins back around and lunges for* PAUL, *getting his hands around* PAUL's *neck to strangle him. It's more than a tussle, this. After a moment it looks like a real attempt to kill. The viciousness and suddenness catch* DANNY *and* GERRY *off-guard. They are, for a second, frozen.* DANNY *screams.* LEN *takes one hand from* PAUL's *neck so that he might use it to throw punches.* GERRY *and* DANNY *rush* LEN *and grab his free arm. They struggle to separate the two.*

How. Vain.

They pull LEN *off. He's done anyway. All four men are breathing heavily.* LEN, GERRY, *and* PAUL *are slowly calming down but* DANNY's *breathing doesn't slow.*

GERRY: Enough of the bullshit. This is how it will all unravel. We didn't come here to fight or to catch up or to console. We've got to come up with a way out of this thing.

LEN: Yeah, yeah.

GERRY: Paul, you go drive by Lionel's house, see if he's back.

PAUL: Okay.

GERRY: And then… whether he's there or not… I don't know.

DANNY, who has stepped back and away from the other three, is starting to shake. He pulls out a chair and sits down. LEN notices something is wrong.

LEN: Danny?

DANNY throws up on himself. DANNY's head falls back, his eyes roll. LEN and GERRY rush to him. DANNY pisses his pants. The fluid stains his pants and runs onto the floor. GERRY steps back in disgust. LEN holds up DANNY's head.

Hey, Danny? How are you, Danny? Danny?

DANNY comes back around.

DANNY: I'm just… nerves.

LEN: Let's get you a place to lie down.

LEN grabs PAUL's windbreaker from the back of the chair on which PAUL had set it and bundles it into a pillow. He puts it on the floor.

LEN puts his arm under DANNY and hoists him up.

DANNY: I have a number of health issues. I'm afraid I haven't taken that good care of myself. If I had one of those…

He runs out of breath.

…one of those medic alert bracelets? It would be the size of a shackle. Talking too much, talking too much…

LEN: You've managed to keep the pounds off.

DANNY: I am light as a feather. You are a wonderful dancer, Lenneth.

LEN: Few people know that about me.

LEN lays DANNY down.

(to GERRY) Get a coat or something, will you.

GERRY: What? Yeah sure.

GERRY gets LEN's raglan.

PAUL: I… I'm gonna… go check.

LEN: Go check. Get your ass back here as fast as you can.

Beat.

Don't run on us!

PAUL leaves. LEN turns his attention back to DANNY.

We gotta get you outta those pants, Danny.

DANNY: No one's ever found that difficult.

LEN starts to undo DANNY's belt. GERRY has come back with a coat, but stands at a distance.

I'm sorry.

GERRY: Don't worry, Danny.

LEN: It's okay.

DANNY loses consciousness. Lights fade to black.

Danny? DANNY!

ACT TWO

One hour later.

DANNY, his eyes closed, lies on the floor, propped up by a pillow fashioned from LEN's jacket. He has LEN's raglan as a blanket. DANNY's piss-soaked pants have been hung up to dry. GERRY sits in a chair. LEN paces behind the two men. GERRY looks through the audience.

GERRY: A person sitting next to you in a theatre, on a plane or a train. Woman in the adjoining office. Grocer. Banker. The assistant deputy minister. They all have a secret, right? They have all done something wrong, something...

GERRY searches for the right word.

..."malfeasant"... about which they have never breathed a word. To anyone.

GERRY turns around in his chair and addresses LEN.

Isn't that true?

LEN: Statistics concerning secrets are notoriously unreliable.

GERRY turns away from LEN and looks forward.

GERRY: And yet, if you're caught, you can expect no sympathy from your fellow sinners.

LEN checks that GERRY and DANNY are not looking and then surreptitiously takes a small bottle of prescription medicine (he told DANNY he had nothing) from his trouser pocket, opens the top, gets a pill, pops it, and puts the bottle away.

Everybody has done something they know isn't right. Even if just once, so they get the hot, burn-your-fingers feel of it, the queasiness of it... but everybody... they all...

LEN: Throw the first stone anyway?

GERRY: Yeah?

LEN: They start pitching them before you can finish saying, "Let he who is without..." Besides, if I'm not mistaken, in that story it's Jesus putting the question, not some thief.

LEN goes to the heavy interior blinds that PAUL had made such a show of closing and opens one so that he can look out. The blue light of the city enters.

What do you teach at the university?

GERRY: History.

LEN: I knew that but I mean… what area of…?

LEN turns back from the window and continues his pacing.

GERRY: I'm a Mesopotamian.

LEN: Oh. Like? Like Iraq?

GERRY: *(wearily)* Yeah.

LEN: Excellent timing.

GERRY: You'd think.

LEN: No?

GERRY: I don't do sound bites. People aren't interested in complexity. They want some "expert" to tell them who's going to prevail, who's going to "win," when you know nobody will.

GERRY thinks.

There is this prick in the department, Archibald hates-being-called-Archie Rumbolt. Archie figured it out. His area is British Colonial India. The Raj. The Mutiny. Raging sepoys at Dum Dum. Of course with it comes some passing knowledge of Afghanistan.

Beat.

Afghanistan up until, at the very latest, World War I.

LEN: The Great Game and all that?

LEN continues to roam the room.

GERRY: Thought you never read the books, Len.

LEN doesn't answer. DANNY opens his eyes.

Does this limitation in Archie's understanding diminish his capacity to pronounce on Afghan affairs? To give good head and shoulders on TV? Not at all. He bold-faces it. No one asks that he know what he's talking about, only that he sounds like he does. Archie is a fraud. Gaming the system he has moved past me in standing at the university. He isn't half the scholar I am. He possesses what I do not: Archie has "certainty." Or at least the sense of it. So now I have to listen to Archie pronounce in those endless committee meetings. And you know what I most want to tell Archie? What I really want to say when I rudely interrupt him, cut him off in the middle of a sentence? I want to say to him and all those other nobs around the table, I want to say, "I stole money from this university. I have so little respect for you and your ilk that I robbed the place; I knocked the joint over. You might be the new chair, you might be the new head of the department, but I… "

LEN passes the tarp-covered table and, struck by curiosity, lifts the tarp. He peers under and laughs.

"I… am a…"

With a great flourish LEN whips off the tarp, revealing an octagonal poker table. The sound interrupts GERRY. The table is purpose built, with a green baize cover, little cup holders and wells with chip holders. Each players setting has a full complement of chips. There are a couple of decks of cards.

LEN: Poker night! Poker night with the boys!

LEN laughs derisively. He picks up a deck of cards. He can cut it with a single hand. He keeps doing this and otherwise manipulating the deck like a sharp.

Paul has a little get-together with fellow "husbands," does he?

GERRY: Yeah.

LEN: Friday night with the boys?

GERRY: Tuesday nights.

LEN: You know about it?

GERRY: Came a couple of times.

LEN: He's never invited me. Friendly game?

GERRY: "Friend" like accomplice?

LEN: Stakes?

GERRY: Table stakes? You buy in for fifty bucks. Tournament hold 'em.

LEN: *(mocking)* As seen on TV.

GERRY: It's a bit of fun.

LEN: The only way to play is for everything you have.

GERRY: I'm not enjoying that much.

LEN: We used to have a game in the science building cafeteria, remember?

GERRY: I do.

LEN: Lionel would play. Paul. You played for everything in your pocket in those days.

GERRY: I had less. I had nothing. You can't make the comparison.

LEN: You're certain you have more now?

GERRY: Actually... if you did a tally, assets and liabilities, I don't know.

DANNY: Despite what they say, less *is* less.

LEN: You would know.

DANNY: Blow me, Lenneth.

LEN: How did Paul find you this evening?

DANNY: I have a fixed address, even if it is just a room. I'm not like a street person.

GERRY *squirms.*

Paul has dropped me off there a few times.

LEN: After a round of golf.

DANNY: I'm not even invited to the poker game. Every year I go up to his house... show up, you know... and offer to rake the leaves. Paul will give me... like three hundred bucks.

GERRY: Good money.

DANNY: You should see the leaves at that place! It's well... it's like a mansion. No, it *is* a mansion.

LEN: I would have thought they'd have groundskeepers.

DANNY: They do. I push a few leaves around, gawk at Paul and Virginia through the windows, take a leak by the jungle gym, get my you-freaked-me-out-please-leave money, and Paul drives me home. The sooner I finish up the better.

LEN: They're happy? Paul and Ginnie?

DANNY: As happy as two rich people with all their teeth can be.

Beat. DANNY surveys the room.

What is this place?

GERRY: A few years ago Paul started his own business. After he and Virginia came back from…

PAUL enters. He's carrying a large paper bag. The bag is covered in a garish print.

LEN: Jesus, where were you?

PAUL: I was talking to Debbie.

GERRY and LEN start with excitement and apprehension.

LEN: Lionel's Debbie?

PAUL: Yeah.

GERRY: You didn't go in the house or anything?

PAUL: No. I'm going to drive by, like you said, and from like half a block away I can see Debbie coming out of the house. She's getting in the car.

GERRY: You followed her?

PAUL: Yeah, it was tricky 'cause I had driven past before she started the thing. I was going as slowly as I could without looking suspicious. I'm looking at her in my rear-view and she's in the car but she doesn't start it.

LEN: The car.

GERRY: What about it?

LEN: Just sitting in it.

LEN turns to PAUL and gestures that he should continue his story.

PAUL: I figured she's got to be going somewhere. I mean she's been at the police station all day. She must…

GERRY: Probably visited a lawyer too.

PAUL: So I drive around the subdivision. I don't know how you do this, like to "tail" someone…

LEN: *(impatiently)* Come on…

PAUL: Ten minutes or so… probably more… I figure I missed her, I didn't want to drive past again, but then I catch her, she's pulling out on to Franklin Avenue. She'd been sitting in that car the whole time.

LEN: She took the time to…

PAUL *has placed the bag he brought on the card table. He opens it.*

GERRY: You followed her?

PAUL *withdraws a bucket of take-out fried chicken.*

PAUL: She got chicken.

LEN *hasn't been able to eat chicken since his summer job at Empire Packers.*

LEN: Chicken.

PAUL: I tried to make it look like it was a coincidence, that I was there…
"gettin' chicken."

PAUL *gestures to the bucket of chicken.*

LEN: She recognize you?

PAUL: I introduced myself and then she remembered.

LEN: Reaction? She freak?

PAUL: No. She seemed distracted, didn't want to talk.

LEN *releases a breath as though he'd been holding it.*

LEN: Then Lionel hasn't sung.

GERRY: No, not necessarily. Maybe she didn't want to talk to Paul because she knew that her husband was, at that very moment, downtown
making a deal with the prosecutor, naming names in exchange for…

GERRY *searches for the word.*

…for leniency.

PAUL: I can't see Lionel doing that.

GERRY: Would you?

PAUL: I don't know.

LEN: I would. I'd sell all of you out in a heartbeat.

DANNY *puts his open hand over his heart and taps out a series of three heart-
beats, six taps in total—"bump-bump."*

DANNY: Heartbeat's up. You'd like to, Len, but you couldn't sell us out.

LEN: Think about this woman's situation. The life they built is going up
in flames unless her husband turns state's evidence. She comes face to

face with one of the suckers. Hubby is downtown giving up to the cops. You think her blood runs cold enough that she can pretend she doesn't know this? She couldn't be that good.

GERRY: She's been with Lionel for years, who knows what he's been up to. She could be Lady Macbeth for all you know.

PAUL: Maybe.

LEN: What did she say?

GERRY: Small talk?

PAUL: At first, like, "Wow, right, Paul," and of course I ask after Lionel.

GERRY: How'd she react?

PAUL: I could see right away she'd been crying, but she seemed on the other side of something. She said that Lionel's business had a few setbacks.

LEN: Setbacks.

PAUL: They were "re-evaluating" and that he, Lionel, had to go away for a while…

GERRY *gasps*.

…but that after that… they… were going to scale back.

LEN: Fuck! Fuck! Fuck!

PAUL: She seemed… she seemed, you know, okay with it.

LEN: You said she'd been crying?

PAUL: I know but… she seemed, I said, "on the other side of something." She seemed relieved. Maybe because something was over.

LEN: There's relief in that, is there? In the end of things?

PAUL: Yeah, sometimes.

GERRY: I guess that's it. I guess Lionel's done.

PAUL: He's got kids.

LEN: Yeah, but it's not like Gerry's situation.

PAUL: What's that?

LEN: There are issues, right?

GERRY: I would rather not, okay.

PAUL: *(to GERRY)* I knew that Brian had…

GERRY: Can we leave it.

DANNY: Someone please tell me?

GERRY: My son, Brian. There are issues. And more with his mother, all right.

PAUL: I didn't know.

GERRY: She's gotten hooked up with these religious… We have differences concerning the correct course of care, okay.

LEN: *(to PAUL and DANNY)* So your whipped default is to let her have her way?

LEN throws the deck of cards he has been holding at GERRY. GERRY jumps to his feet and shoves LEN, hard. LEN staggers slightly.

GERRY: Your rage is boring the shit out of me, Len!

LEN: Acceptance is boring. Obedience is boring.

GERRY: It's more complex, is one thing. Rage is simple.

LEN: *(with derision)* Better to be depressed like poor Paul? Yes I'm angry. What else is there?

DANNY: Action?

Shoving LEN has transformed GERRY. He's looser, physically, as if he's cast off a weight, but he's also jumpier. He's moving about faster, trying to keep up with racing thoughts.

GERRY: Danny's right. I don't want to talk about my life anymore, okay.

(to all) And I don't want to hear about yours. Fuck the band's reunion tour, it's bullshit. We've been wasting time. What are we going to do? DO. DO!

PAUL: If we apologize, without reservations, publicly. We say we are deeply sorry for a youthful indiscretion, that we will pay back the money…

DANNY: They say confession is good for the soul.

LEN: Suppose you haven't got one?

PAUL: Politicians get caught at something, they apologize, they move on. An apology is changing the channel.

GERRY: That's true. Contrition is common currency these days. You couch it in terms of another time, right... you say, "At the time"... and then, "Now, years later, in retrospect." You're sorry for the past. The past.

LEN: You're dreaming now.

DANNY: Are you really sorry though, Paul, that you stole the money, or just that you got caught?

Long beat. PAUL *delivers an absolutely convincing statement of regret. It's a final dress-rehearsal performance for the benefit of the men.*

PAUL: I am genuinely sorry that I misappropriated the funds. If I had my time back I would never, would never have done it. I have prayed...

PAUL *steps out of character for a second and mimes the underlining of the word.*

... *prayed* many times since that I could have that time back, that I could make it right. I am ashamed of my actions. I am ashamed of the embarrassment I have caused my family and my friends. I don't ask for forgiveness, I know it's too late for that. But I will pay back what I took and carry with me, every day, for the rest of my life, as I have carried with me every day since that one error in judgment, a terrible disappointment, a disappointment in myself, over this grave, albeit youthful, indiscretion.

Long beat. PAUL's *tone changes completely, revealing the above to have been a performance.*

Like that.

LEN: That was good, Paul. How many times have you practised that speech on Ginnie?

PAUL: Don't...!

Beat.

There is no shame in apologizing.

LEN: When did that happen? When did the shame come out of apologizing? When did it become self-congratulatory to say you were sorry? When did it become an affirmation?

LEN now makes the repetitive nodding from the waist motion of standing prayer.

I am sorry, sorry, sorry, apologize, apologize, forgive, forgive, forgive,

He stops.

If it would work I would try it. I would. I would. But you know what... I'm only sorry I got caught.

DANNY: Me too, only I'm even more sorry that I got caught than any of you guys. I am sooooo sorry I got caught.

They all wait for GERRY.

GERRY: I am not sorry I stole the money. I mostly wish I'd gotten away with more, with much more. Without any justification at all I feel I deserve that money. It is compensation in lieu of good luck.

Beat. LEN and DANNY cheer.

LEN: YEAH!

DANNY: That's the truth!

LEN: Go ahead, Paul, tell everybody you're sorry, but you might as well stand up and say, "I am ridiculous. Look at me, look at all us, we are ridiculous." Danny had it. "Action."

GERRY: We've got to DO something. Apologizing isn't "doing" anything.

LEN: We go. We go. That's what we said when we did it. We said if we got caught we'd disappear.

PAUL: *(to GERRY)* Exactly how we got in this mess, Len revving us up. "We go. We go."

(to LEN) Too young and naive to see it for what it was.

LEN: But we're not so young anymore. Perhaps, now, we better know how to run. Can do it in the dark.

GERRY: I've lost some speed over the years, Len.

LEN: If you can't run, then you're in a trap. That's a fact. That's an objective assessment of your situation. Trapped.

PAUL: This is such bullshit, Len. Running is a fantasy. You cut yourself off from everyone and everything around you? You do that forever?

LEN: Yeah.

GERRY: It's not just a smaller world than it was back then, Len, it's one world, one place, most of it under video surveillance.

LEN: Yes.

GERRY: So you run. Where to, Huck? They've settled the Territory.

LEN: You go to a place like this, Professor. Not a small place, not necessarily a big place. Because it's one world it's easier to blend in. In one world I hide in plain sight.

GERRY: You become someone else?

LEN: I've been me this long. No problem. I don't see how it's hard to be anyone at all.

This quiets them.

You think the Lexus and the made suit—you think that makes you stand out, conspicuous consumption, right?

He turns to DANNY.

You can blend in with the snow, hare in the snare. You can get lost in the crowd. I *am* the crowd, Danny. Yeah, the situation was different back then, the world was full of nowheres and you could get there and be nobody, but now the world is all anywheres, you go there, to any of them, and you can be anybody.

GERRY: You become someone else. You get a second chance.

LEN: The boys that make the real money in the market know how to profit from crisis. They buy cheap when the gutless are running. This shit we are in now, that is just such an opportunity.

GERRY: Just such a risk.

PAUL: You turn your back on everything, you walk away from family, friends, your profession, your life, your whole life, you never call back, you don't so much as send a postcard?

LEN: Yes. You don't give yourself much of a second chance if you're carrying all the weight of the first.

GERRY: Who gets a second chance? Imagine, another go round.

DANNY: It's great to think about but... for me... if I had it to do over again, I can't be sure I wouldn't make all the same mistakes. I did the wrong thing a lot of times and each one seemed just right. If I look at the rail of coke on the plate, that jar of whiskey… this is what I'm going to do.

LEN's enthusiasm declines.

LEN: I made mistakes looking right at them so I don't know how I could do any better. But I'm gonna try.

PAUL: I wouldn't want to do anything different.

LEN: You are lying to yourself.

There is a long silence as GERRY considers the question. Learning the answer changes him entirely.

GERRY: I didn't make decisions. I just let my life happen to me.

Long silence.

Running though, isn't that cowardice?

LEN: Sometimes it's harder to run than to stay. Maybe it's courageous.

DANNY: When you're really desperate, courage and cowardice are all tangled up in each other.

LEN: Cover your tracks, you live to fight another day.

LEN's cellphone in the inside pocket of his jacket starts ringing. It might as well be the ticking of a bomb. Just as he pulls it out to answer it stops. Then PAUL's cellphone, on a belt clip, starts ringing. LEN only looks at the display.

Unknown number.

PAUL looks at his phone.

PAUL: Unknown number.

Nobody answers. The phone rings until it stops.

Do you suppose that was…?

Now GERRY's phone, in his pants pocket, rings. GERRY looks at his display.

GERRY: Home. It's my wife calling.

The phone continues to ring, a long time, ten times maybe, before it stops. PAUL looks as though he might be sick.

PAUL: Something is happening out there. People are looking for us.

Beat.

GERRY: *(to LEN)* How is it done?

But LEN doesn't know, all he can do is shrug. GERRY looks to DANNY.

(to DANNY) Really, practically, what does one do?

DANNY sits up. DANNY throws off the coat that has been covering him. He's got some nasty scars and bruises on his legs, heretofore unseen. He stands up and shuffles to his pants. Putting the pants on he responds.

DANNY: How should I know? I'm here, aren't I? I never got away.

GERRY: Do you know?

DANNY: You want me to say, like, you fly to some faraway shithole and then on to a place where the crooks have the keys...

DANNY is putting himself together as someone else, illustrating what he is saying as he goes. First he picks up PAUL's windbreaker and dons it.

And I know that some professional hoodlums do actually do that... but... you're no pro, Gerry. With respect... you're just some guy teaching at the university.

GERRY: I know that.

DANNY: Identity. It's on the street now. It's not your spirit, it's... goods. Look how you got into this, with Len walking around graveyards writing down the names of dead babies off headstones.

Beat.

How would *you* really do it? For you to disappear... it's Centreville, it's Cedardale, it's Oakridge Estates.

Now DANNY laughs. He picks up and dons LEN's raglan.

It's the mall for you, Gerry. You have to hide in a lineup at the post office, no one would even notice your face on the wall!

GERRY: Sure.

DANNY: The practical end? You buy a new name from organized crime. You will be some hustler whose body nobody is ever gonna find, some full-time loser who had it coming, some dead junkie—in your next life you could come back as me, sweetheart.

DANNY has walked up to PAUL and now, gingerly, takes the glasses from PAUL's face and puts them on. He has completely transformed his appearance.

You have to change, grow a beard, gain some weight, new glasses, dye your hair… small stuff so that someone walking down the street doesn't… but mostly you have to change who you are, you have to have a new story that convinces… it has be "change we can believe in." You gotta land somewhere big enough that no one will notice; you gotta stay close to the ground; you gotta blend like smoke into smoke…

DANNY *now mimics the man, the nobody that* GERRY *must become. He's walking down a corridor, key in hand.*

You are the man in 303 who keeps to himself.

DANNY *mimics opening the door.*

You're polite but not friendly. You'll feed the neighbour's cat when they are away, pick up their mail, but you would never watch their kid.

DANNY *waves to imaginary neighbours.*

You're never gonna be anyplace there is a risk you'll see someone from your old world, no profs, no former students… you'll be making pizzas, deliveries.

Beat.

You'll be the night watchman. The security guard.

Beat.

You are going to be the kind of person that no one needs to look in the eye. You are gonna be small, quiet, and for a long, long time alone. You are going to be simple, you are going to be humble.

DANNY'S *tone changes. He is less lyrical, graver.*

First step: take a couple of days to empty the accounts, turn what you can into cash, max out your plastic on that part of the trail you want them to find. Go the wrong way first.

GERRY: Like empty the accounts, leave my family destitute?

LEN: Take some "Gerry Time."

GERRY: You'd be one of those people who just doesn't give a fuck.

LEN: One of those happy-go-lucky don't-give-a-fuckies.

DANNY: I'm not telling you to do it.

GERRY: "Do" though. It is "doing."

DANNY: It's "do it yourself."

PAUL marches to DANNY and takes back his glasses, roughly.

PAUL: *(incredulously)* "Go the wrong way first." Did you hear that, Gerry? "Go the wrong way, first?"

DANNY: It's… you know… being a villain… an outlaw… not just the costume, not some middle-class tit posing in a leather jacket at the bars downtown. It's not a tat, it's a knife. Villain! And what would it matter, you'd be putting it all behind, you'd be free.

LEN: Villains are free?

DANNY: I didn't say they were happy. I didn't say they were cozy. I didn't say they slept like babies because their conscience was clear. But villains are free.

GERRY: It's not for someone who's going to worry about what they've done, it's not for a man who has regrets.

DANNY: No it's not. This is for a…

He searches for a word and is pleased by what he finds.

…"frontiersman"…! This is for a man that has decided to turn away from the same bullshit society that put me in jail.

GERRY: *(thinking out loud)* If he doesn't believe… I mean what's worse, the hypocrisy of…?

PAUL: Shut up. You're going crazy. You're just panicking. This is just wrong. Freedom isn't "villainy."

DANNY: I didn't say that. I said villains are free. You're mixed up about freedom… you think that it's a "good" thing, but it's not good or bad… it's just the state you're in.

Long beat.

LEN: Fugitives, first when they bolt, people are always rooting for the cops. "Get him! Get that thieving bastard!" But the longer he evades his pursuers, people switch allegiances, don't they? They say "Can he be the one to do it? Can he be the one that gets away?" And when they've given up the chase, called off the dogs, everybody is rooting for the runner, "Go, man, go." They say, "Run. Run for it. Don't look back." Sure, flight is gutless… but escape? Escape is heroic. You'll be on the other side of the wall the way they all wished they could have dared.

Beat.

DANNY: Old men sing songs about you.

This last line is too much for GERRY.

GERRY: "SONGS?" Please. "The Ballad of Lenneth." Such bullshit.

DANNY: Len's right. What kind of people are for the hounds? I'm for the fox. Always for the fox.

GERRY: It's not like you're the killer, is it? It's not like they want their pound of flesh.

LEN: The money's nothing, it's a pittance. You're the guy that said "I'm picking my shoes up out of this shit. I'm gone."

PAUL shakes his head in disgust.

PAUL: Gone. What a goal, to be gone.

LEN: To stay. What a goal, to be in the same place you started.

DANNY: And if you die out there and they never find your bones, it's as if you never died at all. Legendary.

PAUL: When I grow up I want to be missing and presumed dead.

LEN: You don't get it, Paul. Like you don't get anything. To die alone, that is the bravest thing.

DANNY: Braver than me.

PAUL: Or me. Assholes.

LEN: I want to think I'm brave enough… but I've been known to fool myself.

PAUL: *(dripping sarcasm)* No? You?

GERRY: See… if… if you were really going…

GERRY has a sudden realization. He stops cold before making his point and goes to gather up his overcoat. He has focus; he has cooled down. He doesn't even stop to look at the others, leaving before they even know what has happened.

DANNY: Did… Gerry, just…?

We hear a car start outside. Its lights sweep across the room as it pulls away. The three men left inside are silent for a time. They are trying to fathom what has happened.

LEN: Yeah. And you know something? I knew—KNEW—he couldn't do it. I got it wrong.

DANNY: He...?

LEN: He's gone.

PAUL can't believe it.

PAUL: He is not! He went home. He went to see his wife and his child.

LEN starts laughing. DANNY casually makes his way to the paper bucket of chicken sitting on the poker table. He takes out a piece and tries to eat as much as he can... which is very little.

LEN: We all thought that it was just bullshit, but he was having a serious conversation. He was taking it all in.

PAUL: You think you managed to convince him to throw his life away?

The dialogue should be checkerboarded, overlapping. It should be chaotic, but intelligible.

DANNY: *(overlapping)* We didn't convince him of anything. You convince yourself.

PAUL: *(overlapping)* ...to turn his back on everything to become... what...? A fugitive?

A cellphone rings. It's GERRY's. He's left it behind on the poker table. They all just look at it until it finishes ringing.

DANNY: *(to the phone)* He's not here.

DANNY discreetly pockets GERRY's phone.

LEN: *(to PAUL)* You're just pissed off that you didn't end up running the show. Besides, Gerry having fucked off will make your apologizing all the more craven. He saved his family the trouble. Once the lawyers get a whiff of Ginnie's money... I would pay to be there when you tell Whalen.

PAUL: Virginia married me in the end. Get over it.

LEN: Do you think that I...? Even if I had wanted to I was never naive enough to think that Whalen would allow it.

PAUL: Way to rationalize it.

LEN: No. He needed the right sort of sperm donor, asshole. A nice piece that would match the couch.

PAUL: You don't know the first thing about it. You're the one that knocked up the trailer trash.

LEN: *(quietly)* Fuck you. I was Lynn's mistake, she wasn't mine.

PAUL's cellphone rings. He looks at the display.

PAUL: Unknown.

LEN: Don't.

In a clear act of defiance PAUL quite suddenly answers.

PAUL: Hello.

LEN moves towards PAUL. Is he considering snatching the phone from his hands?

LEN: No!

PAUL: *(to phone)* Lionel?

LEN and DANNY freeze.

Yeah. Yeah, Lionel, I saw her. I was getting some takeout and...

LEN waves his arms to get PAUL's attention.

LEN: *(sotto voce)* Where's he calling from?

PAUL: Lionel, where are you calling from...? My phone says... okay, right. Good thinking.

PAUL listens. PAUL is biting his lip nervously.

We heard, terrible... sure... I talked with Len... yeah, Len... understood... no, he's cool... we can help.

Listening.

No problem. You did... you did the right thing, Lionel. We'll help you out. Okay. Okay, bye.

PAUL lowers the phone.

LEN: Where was he calling from?

PAUL: A bar. That was him earlier, calling from a pay phone.

LEN: Good man.

DANNY: What's going on?

PAUL: He's been charged with fraud. And there are tax problems. It's to do with something he has going now. He said that was all the police wanted to talk about.

LEN pumps a fist.

LEN: Lionel, excellent. Good man.

PAUL: He needs some financial help.

LEN: What are friends for? Hey, Paul?

PAUL: We gotta go get Gerry. Stop him from doing something.

DANNY: Hey… wait now. That was…

LEN: Who says that his going has anything to do with us? Maybe this was just his flight opportunity.

PAUL: It will be another set of questions. We've got to stop him, tell him everything is okay.

DANNY: Everything is okay?

LEN: *(to PAUL)* They'll assume it was to do with his family, his job, his life… his "different life." Didn't you say we could become like "different people at different times." They'll assume he was running away from the autistic kid, the born-again wife…

PAUL: Autistic kid? Brian?

LEN: Or birth defects or something?

PAUL: He's got a learning disability, he's like… dyslexic and Sheila's not "born again," she just started going back to church. I think she's an Anglican.

LEN sees how wrong he got it all.

LEN: He led me to believe…

LEN smiles with a realization.

Gerry can do this… he's gone.

PAUL: Fuck you guys.

PAUL runs from the room. We hear his car door outside open and close and his car tear away from the building.

LEN: Go the wrong way first, Paul.

There is a fair beat of silence.

DANNY: I guess we'll have to write a song.

LEN: Yeah.

Beat.

DANNY: I've been meaning…

LEN: Yes?

DANNY: I want to thank you for that time, it was… and… and you lent me some money.

LEN: No, it was Christmas, Danny. That was a gift.

DANNY: Very generous. I hope, at least, some day… to be in a position to give you a gift.

LEN: Don't worry about it.

DANNY: You're a good man.

LEN: No, not really, but at least there was that.

DANNY: Sure.

Long beat.

LEN: You need some money?

DANNY: I do.

LEN takes out his wallet and withdraws what bills are there. He gives it all to DANNY. The touch of the money, of the soft bills in his hand, energizes DANNY. He cannot help himself from doing a subtle little skanking jig, as though some ska has started playing in his head.

LEN: No "thank yous" please.

DANNY: Right. Thanks though.

DANNY goes to leave. He stops at the door.

You never get away with anything, do you, Len?

LEN *thinks.*

Do you?

LEN *thinks some more. He finally answers. He lies, in an effort to comfort* DANNY.

LEN: Sure you do.

DANNY *smiles at* LEN. *He reciprocates, pretending that he believes* LEN.

DANNY: I believe you.

DANNY *leaves.* LEN *gathers up his jacket and raglan, shaking the dust off them. He puts on the jacket and brushes off more dust. He drapes the raglan over his arm as if to leave but he goes nowhere.*

Lights down to black.

FIN

FEBRUARY
BY LISA MOORE

February was first produced by Alumnae Theatre, Toronto, from September 21 to October 6, 2012, with the following cast and creative team:

Helen: Lavetta Griffin
Cal: John Fray
John: Justin Skye Conley
Louise and others: Kathleen Jackson Allamby
Multiple roles: Trevor Cartlidge
John's former love interest: Victoria Fuller
Multiple roles: Steve Switzman

Director: Michelle Alexander

CHARACTERS

Cal: a twenty-seven-year-old man
Helen: a woman in her early fifties
John: a man in his mid-thirties
Louise
Barry
Red
Coach
Driver
Bartender
Dave
Jane

SCENE I

Two spots come up on stage. There are plain wooden chairs in each spot.
HELEN walks into one spot and JOHN into the other. They each speak to the au-
dience. Their speech sometimes overlaps but they aren't aware of each other.
They are both dressed in black leotards or gym clothes. These neutral outfits
can be supplemented with layers of other costumes that will signal time shifts
and scene shifts. When they leave the stage they take their chairs with them.

JOHN: The scary thing? The most scary thing is you think you'll forget them. Then they'll be gone. That's the scary part. You're responsible, right? What if you forget?

HELEN: I made up my mind is the thing. I didn't hold back. Somehow I came up with this idea. I picked up the idea that there was such a thing as love. And it's like I summoned everything I am, every little tiny scrap of myself, and I handed it over to Cal and I said, "This is yours. Here's a gift for you, buddy."

JOHN: My father was on the *Ocean Ranger*. An oil rig that sank off the coast of Newfoundland in 1982. He died out there. They all died, those men. There were no survivors. We heard about it on the radio. I woke up and I just somehow knew my mother was awake. I don't think I heard her. *(in unison)* I just knew.

HELEN: *(in unison)* I just knew. I handed over my whole self. I didn't say "'be careful with it" because I knew Cal would be careful. I was just twenty years old, and I suppose *(in unison)* I didn't know any better.

JOHN: *(in unison)* I didn't know any better. I was a kid and it frightened me. What if I forget him? That's what I was afraid of. *(in unison)* But you don't forget.

HELEN: *(in unison)* You don't forget. This is what I learned: there's an outside. And I was on the outside. I pretended I was inside for the kids. It was an elaborate piece of theatre. I pretended by starting a business, making supper, doing laundry, putting one sock together with another.

JOHN: Just this little kid, and I really loved my father. You know what I mean? He was something.

HELEN: I wanted to know where he was the night that thing went down. That's what I wanted. Was he in his bunk? Did he get to a lifeboat? It's crazy. But I wanted him to be awake.

JOHN: The lifeboats were crushed, a lot of them. They would have been rushing for the lifeboats but they were smashed up when they hit the water.

HELEN: Of course you die alone. That's what it is, right? Ultimately you're alone.

JOHN: The girls were asleep. I'm the big brother. I mean it was late at night. Gabrielle wasn't even born. I woke up. Something felt wrong. I remember that. What woke me? Maybe it was the radio. They were saying it on the radio. Or maybe it was the phone. *(in unison)* The phone rang.

HELEN: *(in unison)* The phone rang.

JOHN: Somebody phoned. Mom was standing in the window and there was a storm. Everything white. *(in unison)* You couldn't see a thing.

HELEN: *(in unison)* You couldn't see a thing. The sky was white. The street was white. There was nothing.

JOHN: Just completely buried.

HELEN: I heard a metal lid. The lid to a garbage tin, gone in the wind.

JOHN: They were out in that. No land, no nothing.

HELEN: I didn't want Cal to be asleep. Playing cards. I imagined that. 120s. Poker. A few guys. Friends. I wanted to be with him.

JOHN: I just remember sitting on a chair in the living room, this was days later. This was when we knew.

HELEN: It must have been a void. Like dying in a void.

JOHN: I was ten. Terrified I would forget him.

HELEN: Three kids and a baby coming.

JOHN: You don't forget. I'm here to tell you. It all becomes more present. More vivid. The things you remember.

HELEN: I needed to see it. I just needed to see it.

JOHN: And now I've got this thing. I've got this thing. Listen. I'll deal with it. That's what I do. I deal with things. This is just one more thing.

JOHN and HELEN stand and move chairs to opposite ends of the stage. The stage is dark.

SCENE II

There's the sound of crashing waves, a storm out to sea. There is static like a radio but the speech is garbled, then alarm bells and the roar of a plane taking off, church bells and then a phone. Stage right a lamp snaps on beside a bed. We see that there's a wooden manikin with a wedding dress on it. And there are two other gowns draped over a nearby chair. HELEN sits up in bed, disoriented, awakening with a start. She's wearing a black eye mask to help her sleep. She rips it off and tosses it to the floor. There's a moment of silence and then the phone rings again and she picks it up. She's hoarse and panicked.

HELEN: Hello, hello, what's wrong, who is it?

There is the roar of a plane taking off. JOHN is stage left, in an airport, standing with his back to the audience. A very red light bleeds up from the ground, as though JOHN is standing in front of a giant window and a red sun is rising in front of him. The sounds of airport announcements flood into the space. He is gradually bathed in the red light that turns golden, and finally an ordinary daylight as he speaks on the phone. He turns to face the audience as he talks. He's holding an uncooked turkey in his arm, like someone holding a baby. He struggles to hold it more comfortably while talking into the phone.

JOHN: Mom.

HELEN: Johnny?

JOHN: What time is it there?

HELEN: Where are you? My Christ. Where are you?

JOHN: I'm in Singapore airport. There's this gorgeous sunset. Or sunrise. I don't know if it's a sunset or a sunrise. I fell asleep on the plane somewhere over the Pacific. I don't know what time zone I'm in.

HELEN picks up her watch. She gradually raises her voice, afraid they have a bad connection.

HELEN: It's three o'clock in the morning.

JOHN: I'm heading back from Tasmania. On my way home via Heathrow. But I fell asleep on the plane and now I don't even know what day it is.

HELEN: What the hell, Johnny?

JOHN: Middle East on business, hopped over to Melbourne and I decided I'd take a look at Tasmania. It was there, right? Thought I'd check it out. What a spot, Mom.

HELEN: You nearly frightened the life out of me, John.

There's a silence between them.

John?

JOHN: It could be Tuesday or it could be Wednesday, I have no bloody idea.

HELEN: Have you got a tan? Johnny, did you get any colour?

JOHN: Mom, you're kind of shouting. I can hear you. You don't need to shout. The weather was fabulous. There was a beach that went on forever, basically, and the sand was white as snow. The air is so clear. It clears your head. You can see for miles. You would have loved it there, Mom. If you'd ever get your arse on a plane.

HELEN: People aren't meant to fly, John. Birds are meant to fly.

JOHN: I did a zip ride, do you know what that is, a zip ride? Talk about flying. I'd like to see you on one of them. That'd be good. You've got a harness and you basically jump off a cliff and you're sailing over a tropical rainforest. The adrenaline. Mom?

HELEN: Are you all right, Johnny?

JOHN: I've got a job interview. I'm coming home for an interview. I'm going to be there in a couple of days. This is it, Mom, this is the one. This is the one.

HELEN: Johnny. That's so great. That's wonderful, honey. You're coming home.

JOHN: Just for the interview. This is a job you got to move a lot. Image consultant for an outfit called Shoreline. I'll really be able to do the stuff I want to do. And I'll be home in time to do the turkey for New Year's Day. I'll be doing my thing, you know, with the turkey. Everything organic. All the fixin's. The gravy. Invite the girls.

HELEN: But are you all right? You sound funny.

JOHN: I don't sound funny. I'm fine. I'm wonderful. I met a girl a while back and we had a bit of a thing.

HELEN: You met somebody? Johnny. That's wonderful.

JOHN: It was just a little thing, a while back.

HELEN: You met somebody though. Is she nice? What's she like?

JOHN: Nice? She was nice. She is nice. She hung up on me.

HELEN: What are you talking about she hung up on you?

JOHN: I got this call and I guess it didn't go very well. I didn't even know she had my number, to tell you the truth. We hadn't really left it like that. I mean it was a fantastic weekend. A week actually. Five or six days. But I thought we said our goodbyes is what I thought. I mean I was pretty clear. Right from the get-go. Just totally honest, up front. She was doing her own thing. She had a thing. I mean we both have things. This was Reykjavik. You have to go there, Mom. There's light twenty-four hours a day. It's fantastic. But I guess the other side of that is darkness.

HELEN: Darkness?

JOHN: I wasn't there for the darkness part of it.

HELEN: What kind of thing? What is your "thing," John? She hung up on you?

JOHN: She said she was pregnant. She said I got her pregnant.

JOHN hefts the turkey up on his hip.

HELEN: Johnny. Johnny.

HELEN throws off the covers, sits on the side of the bed.

JOHN: She phones out of the blue. I didn't even know she had my number.

HELEN: A baby. There's a baby coming.

JOHN: I didn't even know where she was when she called. Like she was in Reykjavik for some academic conference or something, then she was going back to Calgary or Winnipeg or some other infinitely flat place. I can't even remember.

HELEN: You're going to be a father.

JOHN: We had this really nice dinner, just outside of Reykjavik. It was lamb and wine, asparagus, the whole thing. One of those places, you know it's expensive because most of it is plate. Miles of white plate and then you come across a lone carrot or something. You're sitting there, mountains, glaciers, what have you, the light, this incredible light, eating lamb in this really fancy restaurant. I expensed it. I ask a girl out, I pay. She doesn't have to pay. I pay. That much is true. And we went back to my room. Okay? We did. Yes. That happened. And, it's true, absolutely. We had a really good time. Spectacular time. Fantastic. And there had been a lot of wine, like I said, and I guess I wasn't thinking that way.

HELEN: You weren't thinking what way?

JOHN: I wasn't thinking of her cycle or whatever. Jesus Christ.

HELEN: What did you say to her?

JOHN: Mom, it kind of took me by surprise, you know? The accusation. You're the dad. Guess what, you're the dad. You know what I mean? Where did she even get my number?

HELEN: What did you say? John, what did you say to her?

JOHN: Mom. I said. What do you think I said? I said, "Is it possible, maybe, to get an abortion." That's what I said. I said, "Why didn't you get an abortion?" I said something like that. I wondered about the logic of going ahead with a pregnancy. I wondered, I guess, if that was really fair to the father. Whoever the poor bastard is. This was a couple of days in Reykjavik eight months ago. No, Jesus, like, eight and a half months ago. I mean, listen. What was I supposed to say?

HELEN: Eight months ago. John. You asked about an abortion after eight months?

JOHN: I wasn't thinking. Somebody calls you up.

HELEN: *(wearily, half to herself)* Somebody with whom you've slept—

JOHN: Somebody with whom you were perfectly clear. A quick fling. Go our separate ways. I thought she was on the pill. This is a legal issue. Or it could be. I don't even know what my rights are in this situation. I said, you know. A brief encounter, I said. I asked her. I said. I had to ask. I said: "How do you know it's mine?"

HELEN: Nice. Is that the way you were raised?

JOHN: I asked her how she got the bloody number is what I asked her. Anyway, she hung up. Mom... Mom? Mom?

They have been disconnected. He sits down, puts his head in his hands. HELEN *gets out of bed, the receiver pressed to her chest. She stands like that for a moment.*

SCENE III

The stage goes black and two phones ring at the same time. One ring is a cellphone Star Wars *theme. The other is an old-fashioned ring.* HELEN *sits up in bed and answers the phone.* JOHN *also answers the phone. When* JOHN *says "Hello" the stage goes dark on his side. On* HELEN's *side of the stage it's 1982. We know the change in time because the light is a different tone for the past. The light has a warmer, yellowish tone in the past and a slightly cold, bluish tinge in the present.*

HELEN: What? Who is this? Louise. What are you saying? On the radio? This is on the radio? My God. My God.

HELEN gets up and flings open the bedroom curtains and there's a storm outside. We see a video of a wild snowstorm. She turns on the clock radio and we hear a newscast about the Ocean Ranger *experiencing difficulty, that they're out of contact and supply vessels are headed their way. She is frozen in front of the whirling snow. She stares out the window. There's the sound of a snow-plow alarm bell, and the amber light of the alarm coming through the window, the howling wind. We see she is frightened. Young* JOHN *(aged ten) appears in the bedroom doorway, carrying a* Star Wars *lightsaber.* HELEN *turns off the radio.*

JOHN: Mom, what's wrong.

HELEN: What? Johnny. Nothing, honey. Mommy's just. Why are you out of bed?

JOHN: I heard the phone.

HELEN: It was just Aunt Lou.

JOHN: Why was Aunt Lou phoning?

HELEN: Come over here. There's a big storm. That's all.

JOHN: Don't be scared. I'll protect you.

She holds onto him; the lights fade.

HELEN: Something is going wrong, Johnny. Out on the rig. I'm frightened for Daddy. I'm really frightened here, John. I'm really frightened.

SCENE IV

HELEN is standing at the kitchen table, peeling potatoes. Her father-in-law is sitting at the kitchen table.

DAVE: Where are the children?

HELEN: I sent them over to the neighbours. They're over there watching TV.

DAVE: I wanted to catch you, Helen.

HELEN: I'm here.

DAVE: It gave me a turn, I'll tell you that much. Seeing him.

HELEN: You came straight over here after that?

DAVE: It was Cal. I wanted to say to you. You don't want to go over there, Helen. It was Cal. I just kept thinking about all the things. When he was a boy. The things he did or said. I could see it all. It was like watching a movie but nothing moved. This is an awful thing. I'll tell you that.

HELEN: You shouldn't have gone by yourself, Dave. You should have come and got me. I could have had someone watch the kids.

DAVE: It wasn't like a photograph. I don't know what it was like. A photograph doesn't have duration. It doesn't unfold. This seemed to be unfolding. It was him, all right. They had bodies down there with just their ordinary clothes. No survival suits, nothing. And a few men who weren't even fully dressed, like they'd just left their bunks and there were some had their eyes open. I wanted to catch you.

HELEN: I'm here.

DAVE: Because I don't think you should go over. It's up to yourself. But I said to Meg. I said to his mother. I said. "I don't think Helen needs to go over there." She's lying down, Meg is. She's gone in on the bed. She's got the curtains drawn in the bedroom. She still has her shoes on. She didn't take them off. You walk in there and you're not likely to forget what you see. That's what I'm saying, Helen.

HELEN: I might go over, Dave. I might have to. I feel like I need to see him.

DAVE: They looked alive, those men; I half expected them to move. One of them, in particular, it seemed like he was looking straight at me.

HELEN: Cal couldn't swim, that's what I keep thinking about. Was he dressed? Did he have a coat on or anything?

DAVE: He had his reading glasses. They were in his breast pocket. You don't want to go down to see the body, Helen. That's what I came over to say. Only twenty-two bodies. You don't want to see him. I wanted to catch you before you left the house.

HELEN: I'm here.

DAVE: I took hold of his hand, Helen. His hands were there under the sheet. He still had his wedding band on. It's a cold place.

HELEN: I might have to go over, Dave. I have to decide on that one.

DAVE: I got this for you. I said to the man there, "His wife will want that band." The man slipped it off for me and I put it in my pocket. I said: "His wife will want that." I knew you'd want it. Here it is.

DAVE puts the ring on the kitchen table.

I said goodbye to him, Helen. I reached in and took his hand out and I held onto it. That may seem foolish. I mean I spoke out loud in that place. I wanted to say goodbye.

HELEN puts the peeler down and wipes her hands in her apron.

HELEN: It doesn't seem foolish. Holding his hand and saying goodbye. That doesn't sound foolish at all.

HELEN picks up the ring and holds it in her fist near her chest. Lights fade to black.

SCENE V

And we hear, in the dark, a banging rhythm, not immediately recognizable, but as it gets faster and faster we recognize it as the rhythm of a headboard banging against a wall as HELEN and CAL make love. Another banging joins in the first, the banging on the ceiling of the neighbour from upstairs. At first HELEN and CAL don't notice it.

HELEN: God oh God. Holy God.

The headboard slamming hard against the wall.

Oh God, God. Thank you, God, thank you, thank you.

They stop.

CAL: What are you thanking God for? Didn't I have something to do with it?

HELEN: Dear God.

CAL: *(yells to the ceiling)* Sorry, Mr. Doyle. Sorry about that, sir.

HELEN: *(to the ceiling)* Sorry about that. Sorry.

CAL switches on the bedside lamp and the lighting is the rich, yellow light that indicates the past: early 1980s. CAL sits up, his back to the audience. The kitchen table has been removed and HELEN's bed is centre stage.

Oh no, it's four o'clock. I'll be hungover with all them sewing machines going at work eight thirty tomorrow morning. The racket.

CAL: I got to go up to that bloody office again tomorrow. I hate going in there. Feels like I'm going with my cap in my hand. That bastard behind the desk. Doesn't even look up at me. How many of them resumés am I after handing into them.

While HELEN talks CAL sits up in bed, his back to the audience. He removes a condom, holds it under the light.

HELEN: You just keep trying, Cal, that's all. You just keep going up there and they'll hire you just because they're sick of looking at you. Jesus, the paycheques from that rig. I never heard tell of it before. One of the girls in the shop, her boyfriend got on. It's a fortune, Cal. It's a fortune. I'm going to see if she'll get her boyfriend to say your name up there.

CAL: It's all about who you know. You can put what you like on a resumé. Doesn't make no difference to them. None of them are trained, the ones they're hiring. None of them knows what they're doing.

HELEN: If you got on there we could tell Crazy Carl's they can shove their no-money-down, nine months interest-free. I mean in nine months we could have a down payment. We'd qualify for a mortgage if you got on the rig. Imagine what it would be like not to be counting up weeks all the time. *How many weeks have you got?* That's all anybody ever says to each other at the shop. If we had that kind of money, Cal, maybe I could open my shop. Maybe design things. That's what I'd like to do. I've been trying out a few little things, drawings I done. A little dress I designed myself. I think I could have a little business.

CAL: It broke.

He holds up the condom.

HELEN: What?

CAL: There's a hole in it. It broke.

HELEN: Cal. That doesn't happen. You'd want to have awful bad luck for that to happen.

CAL: It happened.

Lights go out.

SCENE VI

The stage is dark. The blue-tinged light of the present. We hear the sound, rising in volume, close to deafening, of JOHN on the zipline flying through the air, and a video shot from the point of view of a person on a zipline. Then JOHN crashes to the stage, and the video turns off. Lights up.

JOHN: God. Oh holy God, thank you, God, thank you, God.

JOHN crashes and rolls and stands up, and pumps his fist in victory. He's wearing a helmet. He does a mock slow-motion Rocky jog in a circle, half singing the theme—Da-da-daaa, da-da-daaaa—arms above his head. He remembers the helmet, takes it off.

Yes. Yessss. Holy God. Yes. Jesus.

Slowly it dawns on him what he's done, that he's flown over a mile, fallen from a great height, that he might have died. He's still in the harness. He becomes frightened, starts to shiver a little. He sits down and draws in his knees and rocks. He hugs himself. He wipes his eyes hard, as if he doesn't want to discover that he's started to cry. He will wipe his eyes in the same way HELEN will in the following scene. His phone starts ringing. It's the Star Wars theme ring. It startles him. He lays it on the ground. It stops ringing and then it starts up again. He answers.

Hello? Who? I'm sorry? Jane? Oh Jane from Iceland Jane. That Jane. The Blue Lagoon, right? Sure I remember. Wow. Yeah. I didn't expect. Yes, I'm good. I'm good. I'm okay. Actually. I'm all right. Unbelievably. I'm really good. Really fucking good. Long time no hear. What was that, like a year ago? Oh. Yeah, I guess, eight months. And a week? Okay. Well, I got a few minutes, sure. What a surprise. But listen, I'm curious. How did you get my number? Kind of tracked me down, hey? Nice to catch up though. Like I said, I've got a few minutes. How are you? What's new since Iceland?

Lights down.

SCENE VII

Yellow lights of the past. LOUISE appears on stage and pulls up the two chairs from the opening scene. They represent the front seat of a car. LOUISE is in the driver's seat. She tilts the rear-view, straightens an eyebrow. HELEN sits in the passenger seat. They have just been to Pier 17 to view CAL's body. LOUISE has driven HELEN home, but HELEN hasn't got out of the car yet. She's gathering her strength. LOUISE takes out her cigarettes and searches in her purse for a light.

HELEN: Thank you, Louise.

LOUISE: Not a problem.

HELEN: Should have got my licence.

LOUISE: You're going to be all right, Helen. I'm glad you didn't go in there.

HELEN: I don't know.

LOUISE: We should have stayed home. Can I come in and make you something?

HELEN: You see that in the mailbox, Louise, that red envelope?

LOUISE: What's that? That's a Valentine.

HELEN: Cal was a great one for marking an occasion with a card and he likes it to get there on time.

There's a horn blasting behind them. LOUISE adjusts the rear-view to look back. First there is one loud horn, then other horns join in.

LOUISE: Go around me, you bloody fool. Look at this guy. Go around.

HELEN: I know what's on that card, Louise. XO, XO Cal. I got a stack of them in the top drawer of my dresser. There's a poem or whatever. He'll have written my name on the top of it. Just one of them poems. Dear Helen.

Horn honking, more aggressive now. From off stage we hear one of the drivers. Finally LOUISE *has found a light. She is about to light the cigarette but hesitates.*

DRIVER: Hey, get going. Move it along, lady.

HELEN: I bet he paid a full dollar for that card. I don't think I can get out of this car, Louise.

LOUISE: This is—I'm trying to quit here.

HELEN: Cal was big on cards.

LOUISE: I don't think Frank ever bought a greeting card in his life. We don't do cards.

HELEN: Flowers. When the kids were born there was twelve roses.

LOUISE: Flowers Frank does. He does flowers. He does the barbecue.

The horns have grown louder.

HELEN: Cal was always saying he'd teach me to drive. He said there might come a time. And now look. What's going on back there? They want us to move. I'm not sure I can move, Louise.

LOUISE: I'll teach you to drive.

HELEN: Oh yes. That'd be good. Patience is your middle name. I can see it now.

LOUISE: Frank then. Frank'll teach you.

HELEN: People say it's no good to get your spouse. But Cal would have been able to teach me. I was afraid, see, Louise. All that machinery in a car. All that metal. You forget how dangerous it is. Now look at me. I just couldn't go in there, Louise. I couldn't see him like that.

LOUISE: You didn't need to go in, honey.

HELEN: People say if you have the body it's real. But it feels real already, I'll tell you that.

Both women turn in their seats and look backwards. Then they turn forward and an irate driver shows up. He trots up behind them in a rage and approaches LOUISE'S *window.*

DRIVER: Lady, you are blocking the goddamn road.

LOUISE: Can you not go around me? Banging on the horn. Go around. Go around.

DRIVER: Lady, look behind you, for the love of God. You've got traffic backed up halfway to Pier 17. I can't go around you. The street isn't plou-wed. There isn't enough room. How can I go around you? And I can't back up because there's traffic all the way back to Bowring Park.

LOUISE: I don't know what I'm doing with this cigarette. I don't even smoke. Every one of them is a nail in your coffin.

She puts the cigarette and lighter away.

DRIVER: Lady. I don't know what you're doing either. Maybe you have all the time in the world, but I've got to get to work.

LOUISE: We were just up to Pier 17. My sister here, her husband was on the *Ocean Ranger*. We were just up identifying the body. But she didn't go in. I just drove her down. The roads are so slippery. I said, "I'll drive you. Nothing is plowed. There isn't a sidewalk." I said, "I'll bring you down there if you want to go." She said she wanted to go, and I said, "I'll come and drive you." But she didn't go in.

DRIVER: I should help you.

LOUISE: Oh we're fine. We're just worn out, is all. You're fine, aren't you, honey?

HELEN: We don't know what we're doing here, sir. I'm just taking a little rest here, I guess. I feel like it would be an awful effort. Just to get out of the car. I mean, I have to get out of the car, Louise. I can't just sit here. Sir, there's a Valentine in the mailbox there. My husband sent it so it would be here more or less on time. He knew he was going to be out on the rig for Valentine's. It's just a card, there's nothing on it really. I should go, Louise. I've got to go inside the house.

DRIVER: Let me help you.

He goes around to HELEN's side and helps her out.

HELEN is digging in her purse for the keys. She goes a bit limp, but the guy catches her. He holds her up a bit and takes the purse and digs for the keys and finds them and gives them to her.

HELEN: Sorry about that. I'm a bit light-headed. I haven't had much to eat. The idea of food. And I'm supposed to be eating for two. But I keep forgetting. What did I have? A piece of toast. It was a job to get that down, to tell you the truth. I feel so light, like there's nothing left of me.

LOUISE: I'll call you.

HELEN: Call me.

LOUISE: I'll call. Are you all right?

DRIVER: She's all right. I'll get her settled away.

HELEN: Give me a call.

LOUISE: I'll call you.

HELEN: You know, it was like I just summoned up every little scrap of myself and I handed it over to him. Like I got this idea somewhere, that's what love is. You don't hold back. I said, "Here's a gift for you, buddy."

DRIVER: I'm sorry for your trouble, missus.

HELEN: I didn't say "be careful with it" because I knew Cal would be careful. I was just twenty years old, and I suppose I didn't know any better.

SCENE VIII

Lights come up on the bedroom but it's a hotel room now. HELEN is wearing a wedding dress. CAL has on a powder-blue velvet wedding suit. They burst into the room together. He's chasing her and she leaps onto the bed and jumps down and runs around with her wedding dress bunched up under her arms and her veil trailing behind. She pushes him away long enough to stamp out of the dress. She dives onto the bed with him. He pulls a cork out of a bottle of champagne. It spurts up and he puts his mouth over it and drinks and passes it to her. They are skylarking. Then HELEN stands up near the window and removes her veil.

CAL: Let's get a shower. Come on.

CAL moves off stage into the bathroom. We hear the shower running.

HELEN: Cal, you can see the whole city. The harbour. Everything. You can see all the way out to Mount Pearl.

CAL calls from the bathroom, the door ajar.

CAL: Lots of goodies in here. There's a little mending kit. They must of known you were coming. Some of those little shampoo bottles.

HELEN: It's beautiful. I'm glad we're so high up. You can see the whole world.

He comes out of the bathroom wearing a shower cap and bathrobe. He tosses another robe to her.

CAL: The water's hot enough to scald the arse off ya. Look, somebody left their bathrobes.

HELEN: Yes b'y. Don't be so foolish.

CAL: Here, I'm taking these. Put 'em in my bag.

He tosses her hotel shampoos and soaps.

HELEN: What do you want that for?

CAL: Souvenirs, b'y.

HELEN: What time do we have to get the car back to your parents in the morning? Your father's going to need the car for work.

CAL: They said we could sleep in. Dad's taking a taxi. Splurging. Come into the shower. Come on, I want to try out me new hat.

He snaps the shower cap.

HELEN: Well, we better put some gas in it. I don't want to give it back empty. Again.

CAL: Come into the shower, have a shower with me. Come on. It's hot and steamy in there.

HELEN: Cal, you're not disappointed, are you?

CAL: Baby. How could I be disappointed?

HELEN: I know you would have liked to wait. I know that.

CAL: This is fine. What? Oh, come on now, don't cry. Helen.

HELEN is sitting on the bed, her arms wrapped around drawn-up knees.

HELEN: Sorry. Hormones, I s'pose.

CAL: This is what I want. I want you. I want to spend my life with you.

HELEN: But you wanted to wait for a family, didn't you? You could have waited, if it was up to you.

CAL: It was a little faster than I thought it'd be, that's all. I mean we didn't plan for it. No house. No job. No stamps. No nothing. You working in that tailor shop. Minimum wage. Jesus anybody would be worried. But the job will come through, Helen. Your friend is after mentioning me, right?

HELEN: Yeah, he said to buddy.

CAL: He said my name.

HELEN: Yeah, he said your name.

CAL: Well, there you go, see.

HELEN: Because, Cal. I knew the minute I laid eyes on you. I knew. I was almost in a panic every time you came into Browned Off. Trying to see if you were with somebody. And when you did come over to talk, I didn't know what to be saying. My face getting all hot and red every time. Everything that came out of my mouth was stupid.

CAL: I know what I got, Helen. Believe me.

HELEN: I hope it's a boy. I hope it's a boy just like you, Cal. That's what I hope.

Lights out.

SCENE IX

A Star Wars *lightsaber whirs through the dark with its sound effects. It's late at night and a young HELEN is in the living room. She is very pregnant. JOHN, aged ten, swishes the lightsaber back and forth around the edges of the living room as if protecting her from unseen terrors. He was by her moaning and has come into the living room to see what's wrong. HELEN is in labour. She lowers herself onto the floor. She is trying to breath through the contractions.*

HELEN: *(whimpering)* I can't do this. I can't. I can't do this.

JOHN: Mom, what's wrong? You have to get up. We have to go. We have to go to the hospital.

HELEN: Aunt Lou is coming, Johnny. She'll be here in a minute. You have to wait here while I go to the hospital, okay? Mrs. LeGrow is coming over to stay with you and the girls. Aunt Lou will be here in a minute. Where the hell is she? Louise? Where are you? Mommy's going to be all right. And when this thing is over. You'll see. We'll have a little baby. You're the man of the family, Johnny. You're my guy. Oh God, oh God. Just come here and hold my hand for a second, will you. Holy God. I don't know if I can do this. I can't do this without your father. Where's your father? Where is he, God? Where is he? Where is he?

LOUISE *bursts into the room. She turns on the lights, the yellow light of the past.*

LOUISE: Helen, no. Helen, listen. You're too early. What are you? Almost a week. Helen, no. You have to wait. Where are your socks? You don't even have any socks on. You're not ready.

HELEN: They're wet. We have to go.

LOUISE: Why are your socks wet? This is my lucky day, this is. Not a bloody sock to be found.

HELEN: They're in the washer, Louise. This baby is coming now.

LOUISE: Let's just put them in the dryer, Helen. I'm going to put them in the dryer.

HELEN: Forget the socks, Louise.

LOUISE: They can't all be wet. Where are they? Where are all the socks? Where are the goddamn socks, Helen?

HELEN: We have to go, Louise. We have to go now.

LOUISE: Johnny, in the car.

HELEN: He's not coming, Louise.

LOUISE: I'm sure as hell not going with you by myself.

JOHN: I want to come, Mom. I'm coming.

LOUISE: Grab your mother's coat, honey. Come on, help me get her in the car.

HELEN: Stay here, John. Just stay here.

JOHN: I want to come with you. Don't leave me here.

HELEN: Louise, don't let him leave this house.

LOUISE: Get in the car, Johnny.

SCENE X

When the lights come up a young JOHN *is standing next to his aunt* LOUISE. *The bed has been surrounded by a white hospital curtain. They are watching the shadows on the curtain leap and fall.* LOUISE *has her gloves in one hand. There are screams from behind the curtain. The voices of doctors and nurses, encouraging* HELEN. LOUISE *holds* JOHN *back. He still has his* Star Wars *lightsaber.*

HELEN: Help me. Help me. Please help, please, somebody help me. I want my husband, I want my husband. Cal?

LOUISE: Come on, Johnny. Let's go downstairs and have a doughnut or something. They got a Tim Hortons near the lobby.

JOHN: I don't want to go, Aunt Lou.

LOUISE: Me neither.

JOHN: I'm afraid.

LOUISE: Me too. But that screaming, that's perfectly normal.

JOHN: It sounds like she's dying.

LOUISE: It's like dying, but it's much worse.

JOHN: Is she going to die?

LOUISE: She'll be wishing she could die right about now, but no, no such luck.

HELEN *gives a last groan. Then we hear the baby crying, and the voices of the doctors and nurses.*

NURSE: Good job, Mrs. O'Mara, it's a little girl. Ten fingers, ten toes.

JOHN *and* LOUISE *are still standing outside the curtain.* LOUISE *goes forward and pulls back the curtain and exits.* HELEN *is still wearing her black eye mask from the first scene. She whips off the mask that has been sitting on top of her head and throws it to the ground in disgust. The lights shift to the blue-tinted light of the present. The young* JOHN *exits. A red sunset comes up on the adult* JOHN *back in the airport in Singapore.*

SCENE XI

HELEN: Hello?

JOHN: What happened?

HELEN: I don't know, we got disconnected.

JOHN: I lost you there.

HELEN: It's this bloody cordless, the battery died. Or that thing you're on.

JOHN: It's a cellphone, Mom.

HELEN: I know what it is.

JOHN: A cellphone.

HELEN: You were gone. The line was dead. You're so far away. I don't think you could be any farther away, could you?

JOHN: Mom, I'm not doing this thing. And I want your support. I'm calling you for support, basically. You should stand by me here. That's your place in this thing. You're my mother. Don't you get that?

HELEN: I get it, John. I'm your mother. That's exactly it, that's the thing right there. I raised you. I raised you by myself.

JOHN: Why can't you say what I want you to say?

HELEN: Listen, this is a baby we're talking about. This isn't something I can fix. You're going to be a father. It's already done.

JOHN: Instead you're taking the side of some woman you've never even met. I have a job opportunity here. Do you understand that? I'm being fast-tracked. The opportunities are staggering right now. This is something I've worked for. You have no idea how far I've come. No idea.

HELEN: A job? And what kind of job is it, John? Listen here, my son, you better think about what you're turning into, what you're going to become.

JOHN: What I'm going to become? What about you? What are you becoming? You never go out, you never meet people. You could be dating. Meeting men. Plenty of Fish, or the other one.

HELEN: The Internet?

JOHN: eHarmony. Mrs. Bursey.

HELEN: Your grade eleven teacher?

JOHN: She met someone on a dating site.

HELEN: Oh yes, I met him. He's a catch, he is. Big mouth on him, not a tooth in his head. All about his new barbecue, property values. Practically twice her age. She's just in time to change his diapers.

JOHN: People do that. They get out. They meet other people. Living all alone in that dark hole of a house.

HELEN: It's not dark, what are you talking about?

JOHN: Mother. It's dark.

Lights out.

SCENE XII

HELEN is on a bar stool. There's music in the background, ambient bar noise. There's a young college girl behind the bar talking to HELEN.

BARTENDER: So you have no idea what this guy looks like?

HELEN: Honestly, that's the least of my worries.

BARTENDER: Well you look great.

HELEN: Oh, no.

BARTENDER: Yes you do. You look really hot.

HELEN: Come on now. How old are you? Twelve?

BARTENDER: Twenty-one.

HELEN: And you think I look, you know, okay? For a bar?

BARTENDER: You look lovely. I wish my mother would do what you're doing. I'd love it if she just went out, met people.

HELEN: You know I went into Halliday's today and asked the guy to cube a steak for me. And I just watched that hunk of meat, under that stainless-steel blade. I thought, that could be my heart right there under that blade, chopped up into little cubes. But it's also a thrill. Do you know what I mean? I have to breathe. That's all. We do that in yoga. Put it in a bubble. Deep breathing. Blow a bubble, float your trouble, right? What time is it?

BARTENDER: It's the traffic; the weather is bad.

HELEN: It's nasty out there, isn't it?

BARTENDER: Traffic is all held up. All over the city. Accident on the Outer Ring.

HELEN: He's not coming over the Outer Ring.

BARTENDER: Prince Philip Drive is bad.

HELEN: Because we said eight, eight thirty, so. I mean, I got here early.

BARTENDER: It just started snowing when I came on, but it's really dirty out there now.

HELEN: My daughters said, "Mom, you're not a dinosaur, you know?" "Get out there," that's what they said.

BARTENDER: Of course, why wouldn't you.

HELEN: They said, "Don't put up a picture." They said, "Plenty of time for a picture later."

BARTENDER: Yeah, you don't have to put up a picture. I mean, it's about meeting people, right? It can be a really nice thing.

HELEN: I'll tell you what, not one of my friends would have the guts to do this. I don't have a single friend who would be able to do what I'm doing here tonight. Sit up on a bar stool. Can I have another one of these? What are they again?

BARTENDER: A strawberry-banana cooler.

HELEN: Hit me. Another cooler please? Do you think I've overdone it, with the makeup?

BARTENDER: You look really nice.

HELEN: I struggled to define myself in that profile, and what I wanted in a man. It seemed important to know what was true about myself.

BARTENDER: You can say whatever you like in those things. Beauty of the Internet.

HELEN: I wanted to say what a pleasure my life had been, and that I'd lost something big. I built up a business. I mentioned that. I said I've kept my heart open and it's been a struggle. You have to tell them, in these profile things. You have to kind of sum it all up.

BARTENDER: You felt like you had to be honest.

HELEN: There's other things that are sort of mandatory.

BARTENDER: Like your hobbies or whatever.

HELEN: How old, what movies, what music. I wrote with real honesty.

BARTENDER: Did you say candlelight?

HELEN: I said I candlelight; I said I wanted to hold hands. How humiliating.

BARTENDER: Cooking?

HELEN: And dining out.

BARTENDER: A lot of people say a glass of wine with candlelight.

HELEN: I said a glass of wine now and then. I said I would enjoy maybe we could read to each other. Books. Can you imagine? I said I like to read. Sexy, right? What I should have said was this: I am so bloody lonely it doesn't matter who you are or what you are, I am capable of loving you.

BARTENDER: Most people don't say that.

HELEN: I didn't write that I wanted to have sex.

BARTENDER: You want to stay in your comfort zone. If you have one.

HELEN: I want to have sex, believe me, but I didn't write that. What I wanted to say was I am capable of making love to you in such a way that you will remember it for the rest of your days. I am capable of giving that kind of pleasure. I am capable of feeling it.

BARTENDER: That would get you a few hits. You'd be tapping into a different demographic there.

HELEN: I said I expected kindness and a sense of humour. But you know what? There was no humour in what I wrote on that profile. No humour at all. I should have said, "Could you be my dead husband for an afternoon? Could you put on his clothes, I still have them? Will you wear the cologne he wore? Will you smoke Export As and burn the steaks on the barbecue and be charming with all my women friends and beloved by all who knew you." That's what I should have said. Young lady, do you have a bathroom in this place?

BARTENDER: It's at the back there, would you like me to…?

HELEN: Yes?

BARTENDER: Call you a cab maybe?

HELEN: Would you do that, dear? I'm just going to freshen up, wash this guck off my face. You know what's the worst thing about all this? He wrote about his plantars warts. He had to go have them frozen off. Or burnt, removed, whatever they do. He was sharing. I mean the poor guy was terrified. Okay, it's true, I was a little on the flowery side, you know. We had lots of emails and I was what you call flowery. But he couldn't spell his way out of a paper bag. King of the emoticon, this guy. Thing was, I wrote right after the day surgery. Fast as I could. Checking every two seconds to see if he was okay. I was all upset about his plantars warts. Concerned for him. That's the most humiliating part. He probably came in here and took one look at this purple coat and walked back out, right?

BARTENDER: Not a chance. It's the weather. He's probably in a ditch somewhere, the lousy bastard.

HELEN: He walked in here and took one look and he saw I was old, that's what happened.

BARTENDER: Nah, it's a wild night out there, it really is. The wind is howling.

Lights down.

SCENE XIII

HELEN is asleep on the bed. CAL is in the bathroom flossing his teeth. He comes in and sits on the bed beside her and she wakes up.

CAL: You should look out the window.

HELEN: What time is it? I must have fallen asleep. I thought you were out on the rig.

CAL: It's late now. It's five in the morning.

HELEN: Did you check on the children?

CAL: The children are fine. It's amazing out there. There's the lid of a garbage tin up in the tree branches across the street. It's a wild night. It really is. I haven't seen anything like it before. Everything is buried. The cars are buried. The garbage buckets are buried. Even the stop sign across the street.

HELEN: What is it, some kind of storm?

CAL: The wind is howling but it's very quiet, Helen. It's completely quiet. There's no traffic. It's pretty amazing.

HELEN: I wanted to tell you something. What was it?

CAL: There was a list on the rig, Helen.

HELEN: I must have fallen asleep. I just lay down for a minute with my book. I've got this really good book. I wonder where it went. I must have dropped it. It was a magnificent story.

CAL: We developed a list out there, a lean. The whole thing started tipping to one side. It was impossible to recover. They sent out a call for help.

HELEN: What are you talking about, Cal?

CAL: You should go to the window. You should see this. It's really something out there. You can't see a thing. You can't see a hand in front of you. It's white out there. It's just white. Everything is buried.

HELEN: I'm cold. I've got the shivers. I must have fallen asleep. I fell asleep with the book in my hands. It was a really good story. I was really caught up in it. It must have fallen between the bed and the wall. It must have gone down in the crack.

SCENE XIV

Lights up on HELEN and BARRY standing in the living room. He's in paint-speckled jeans and a T-shirt with a measuring tape attached to his waistband. He's holding a hammer.

He stamps his foot twice.

BARRY: I'm going to be honest with you. Though you might not want to hear it. Some women don't want to hear this coming.

HELEN: Go for it.

BARRY: What you need here—

HELEN: Yes, what do you think I need?

BARRY: You need a subfloor.

HELEN: A subfloor.

BARRY: You think you can get away without it. I'm only being honest. I could lay down that floor, if that's what you want. It's your house.

HELEN: No, I hear you.

BARRY: I'm being honest with you right now. If I don't put down a subfloor the whole thing is coming back up.

HELEN: Subfloor. Absolutely.

BARRY: You're going to go with the subfloor?

HELEN: I'm going to have to. I have to trust you here. I certainly want a solid foundation.

BARRY: I'm not going to steer you wrong on the subfloor issue, I guarantee you. It's going to cost you.

HELEN: No doubt.

BARRY: But without a solid foundation for your hardwood. See, there's just no point going ahead without a foundation.

HELEN: I want to take out those walls. Maybe that's crazy. But I need to get some light in here.

He's tapping the walls, checking for support beams.

BARRY: Basically you're opening everything up?

HELEN: That's my goal. I need more light. I've been in this house twenty-seven years and it's very dark. It's a dark house. Don't you think it's dark in here?

BARRY: Open concept. You're after a kind of open concept thing.

HELEN: And do you paint?

BARRY: That's something we can discuss later, if you wouldn't mind. I got a lot of jobs coming up. A painter, you could get someone else. This is the season where I'm really busy. Carpenters are in demand, the carpenters do the kind of work I do. There's not too many of them.

HELEN: It's hard to get someone, I know.

BARRY: It's really hard these days. What colour were you thinking, out of curiosity?

HELEN: I hadn't really figured it out yet.

BARRY: Because I'll tell you something right now. I had a woman on Canada Drive had this deep red. Deep red living room. That's a mistake you can't cover. How many coats did I have to throw on that? Didn't matter how many times I painted it, the red bled through. I was at it, I don't know, Jesus, seven coats or something. That's something you'll regret. There are mistakes you can't just walk away from. When this job is done I don't want you regretting anything.

HELEN: So you can do it?

BARRY: You want a foundation, and you want me to knock down some walls. You want to let a bit of light in. I can do that.

HELEN: You're not one of those guys says he's coming but doesn't show up?

BARRY: I'll be here. Don't you worry.

Lights down.

SCENE XV

Lights come up on the living room and HELEN *is sitting at a sewing machine.* BARRY *is setting up at a table saw. The lighting suggests the downstairs of* HELEN's *house has been opened up, and there are more windows. It's brighter. Their movements are coordinated, but they are absorbed in their work and not paying attention to each other. The noises of the saw and the sewing machine seem to be in conversation with each other. When the saw speeds up, so does the sewing machine. Then* HELEN *takes a break.*

HELEN: Sandwich?

BARRY: Sure.

HELEN: Ham and cheese?

BARRY: Yeah, sure.

HELEN: Beer?

BARRY: Yeah, and can you do your pickle thing, the thing you did with the pickles the last time. That was something.

HELEN: You noticed that?

BARRY: And the radish, the way you carved the radish.

HELEN: That was just—

BARRY: It was a nice touch.

HELEN: Just a garnish.

BARRY: Yeah, but you took care with it. I appreciate that. You know?

HELEN: Well you're doing a grand job here, Barry. With this window, the whole room feels bigger. And the wall gone. Funny how fast you get used to it. What, you took that down two weeks ago, and it feels like it's always been this way.

BARRY: Those curtains really set it off, Helen.

HELEN: You were right about the cherry wood for the windowsills.

BARRY: Cost a little more.

HELEN: But it's really warm. It's a warm wood.

BARRY: I learned alongside my father. The first thing I ever built? A little dory. We built a boat together. Everybody knew how to do that back then. Like you were born knowing how to do it. Or you learn watching your father. You get older, it's hard on the back. You can't do it forever, I'll tell you that.

HELEN: You went off to the mainland, did you?

BARRY: Went up to Edmonton. I was up there twenty-five years. I'm telling you, Helen. The money.

HELEN: Place was paved with gold, I s'pose.

BARRY: We were picking it off the trees. I had a guy ask me to build him a mansion in the country by a lake. Black marble floors. Never saw nothing like it. I was working two- or three-month stretches sometimes, without a day off, back then. I took my son back to see that house fifteen years later. Drove up and down the street I don't know how many times, Helen, place was full of houses exactly like it and crowded in on top of each other. I never did find the one I worked on. I'd say Newfoundlanders built half the places up there. I had a little trailer at the time. Go home and stand up over the little sink there in the trailer, open a tin of Vienna sausages. That was supper. Flake out in front of TV, wake up in the chair soon as the sun come up, and back at it again.

HELEN: My husband was on the *Ocean Ranger*.

BARRY: Jesus. I'm sorry.

HELEN: No, no it's okay… let me get you that sandwich…

While HELEN speaks she makes BARRY the sandwich.

You know what gets me about it? What I can't let go of? The men weren't trained. It all started with a porthole, Barry. And that got broken because they never lowered the shutter, the deadlight. A wave of ice smashed through. The metal shutter wasn't drawn down, see. They never followed procedure. The water got in and short-circuited the ballast control panel and the men never knew how to operate it manually. There was a manual, that's it. And they never read the manual. This is what I'm saying. They weren't trained. There were brass rods. And nobody knew how to use the brass rods so the rig developed a list out there. I'm after reading the Royal Commission Report, I got that bloody thing memorized. I wake up in the middle of the night and I know where the bloody rods go. Brass rod, appropriate solenoid valve located under the mimic panel. I know how it works, Barry, I'm after reading through that thing so many times. But they never spent the money to train them. It was all about profit.

BARRY: My God, Helen. I'm sorry.

HELEN: That's why my husband died. Simple as that.

BARRY: I was on the mainland. But we heard about it. I went to school with a fella who was on it. Everybody knew somebody on that rig.

HELEN: A long time ago now, I suppose.

BARRY's cellphone rings.

Feels like yesterday sometimes. Answer your phone.

BARRY: I'm going to have to take this one.

HELEN: No, please, go ahead, answer.

He answers it. He turns his back on HELEN for the phone call. She sits down to sew and makes the machine go furiously loud, to drown him out, but she's also straining to hear, so she stops, adjusts a seam.

BARRY: Hi, how are you? Yeah, I'll be there. I'll pick you up. Wait inside, okay? I don't want you getting caught in the snow. I love you too, honey. Bye now.

(to HELEN*)* I have to… *(gestures with the phone)* I'm going to have to cut out a bit early today if that's okay.

HELEN: Sure.

BARRY: Your husband was a lucky man, Helen.

HELEN: We were kids. Thank you, Barry. For all this.

She gestures to the room.

BARRY: I think it's looking pretty good.

HELEN: Absolutely.

BARRY: Just the trim left now.

HELEN: Then you're done, I guess?

BARRY: Pretty much all done once we get the trim. It's looking really nice. I'll see you, Helen.

SCENE XVI

JOHN comes through the door as BARRY is leaving. JOHN is still carrying the uncooked turkey.

HELEN: John, you're here. My God, you're home.

JOHN: I'm home.

He hugs his mother, turns to BARRY, and shakes his hand.

John O'Mara.

BARRY: Happy to meet you, John. Barry Connors. I'm just on my way. So, Helen.

HELEN: Yes. You'll be back. After your whatever. Your thing.

BARRY leaves and HELEN turns back to JOHN to hug him.

JOHN: I just need a quick change. I have to go immediately. I have to get going, Mom. Right now.

JOHN rushes off stage to the kitchen and comes back with a roaster. He has a bag of dressing. He puts the turkey in the roaster and begins to stuff it vigorously. He stops to tear open his suitcase and pulls out all his clothes.

HELEN: You're going?

JOHN: The interview. The interview.

JOHN goes into the bathroom, comes out with his shirt off. He starts digging through his luggage, throwing out shirts. He finds the one he wants, hands it to her out of the bag.

Can you iron this?

HELEN: Is that all you have to say?

JOHN: Can you iron this please?

HELEN: About the renovations.

JOHN: Oh.

Takes it all in quickly.

Yeah. Nice.

HELEN: There's a lot of light. I mean in the early evening. This whole room. It comes through those two windows. They're brand new, the windows. And the colour. Sail White and the trim is going to be cappuccino, or latte. Decaf latte, something like that. Barry and I figured something light for the walls. This guy Barry, your aunt Lou suggested. He's such a find. I mean you look for a guy these days. Forget it. But this guy's a master carpenter. Very in demand.

HELEN begins to iron the shirt.

I was lucky to get him.

JOHN: Just give me the shirt, that's good enough.

JOHN returns to stuff the turkey. When that's done he tries on a jacket, takes it off, and puts on another.

HELEN: I haven't seen you.

JOHN: But this job, Mom. If I get this job?

HELEN: You just came through the door.

JOHN: Guys would kill their own mothers for this job. This is an opportunity. I mean they have the brand, but I want to look at the company behind the brand, you know what I mean?

HELEN: Have you phoned the girl, John?

JOHN: I know you don't think much of me working for the oil industry. You think you haven't made that good and clear? You and the girls.

You're all against me. Nobody ever says, "Good for you, John." Nobody says a goddamn word.

HELEN: Let's not get into that, John.

JOHN: No, let's get into it. I want to get into it.

HELEN: Have you called that young woman back? Have you made contact?

JOHN: Cathy with her nursing. Nurse Cathy. Lulu with her massage parlour. That' all fine and dandy.

HELEN: It's a health spa.

JOHN: The Chakra Centre. Do you know where some of those chakra points are located? I set her up. I'm the one that gave her the start-up capital.

HELEN: We're all grateful, John.

JOHN: I'm not looking for gratitude, Mom. What I would like? What would be nice around here? A little respect. This job.

HELEN: Image consultant?

JOHN: That just means—

HELEN: I know what an image is, John.

JOHN: I am trying to do things differently. That's what I'm trying to do.

HELEN: We heard it on the radio. That's how we heard your father was dead.

JOHN: Mom. You put that thing in at five hundred for fifteen minutes and then you turn it down. Okay? Don't mess this up, Mom, I'm not kidding. You have to turn it down.

HELEN: You don't manage something like that, John. You don't manage that kind of loss.

JOHN: You turn it down to three fifty. And you baste it. Just, you know, every now and then, check the goddamn thing, okay. Four hours. It's a big bird. Not a minute more.

HELEN: You have to live through it.

JOHN is tying his tie, in a rage now.

JOHN: You drive a car, don't you? You heat your home? Listen, here's the truth. Okay? You want to hear the truth? I work hard and I have fun. That's what I do. And come night, when I'm finished work? I kick back and relax. I eat fantastic food. I drink great wine. I pick up beautiful women. And I show them a good time. It's pretty simple. And you know what? I deserve it.

HELEN: Johnny, you find that girl's number now and you call her back.

JOHN: I've got an interview, Mom.

HELEN: I don't give a good goddamn what you have. You call that woman and apologize. Do you hear me? John? That's what you're going to do.

JOHN: I'm getting a job is what I'm doing. That's, actually, what I'm going to do. Am I responsible, here, for a baby? Is that what you're saying? She made a decision that didn't include me. That was her mistake.

HELEN: You know what it's like to grow up without a father, John.

JOHN: I don't want a baby right now. Does that make me a bad person? I'm the bad guy? I'm asking for your support. Please. Mom. Can you just take my needs into consideration here?

HELEN: John. I want you to consider, just for a moment. How hard it is to be a single mother. Consider that.

SCENE XVII

The lights go down on the living room and come up in the kitchen. It's 1982 again. HELEN is cooking scrambled eggs for all the kids and putting toast in the toaster and making four lunches. She is placing the table. She's dressed in a light nightdress. Young JOHN is bouncing a basketball, a steady beating, loud. She is frantically beating eggs in a chrome bowl. A kettle is coming to a boil.

HELEN: Can you go tell your sisters breakfast is ready and they're going to be late if they don't hurry up?

JOHN: *(shouting)* Breakfast is ready and you're going to be late if you don't hurry up.

HELEN: I could have done that myself. Remind me to sign Cathy's permission slip.

JOHN: Sign Cathy's permission slip.

HELEN: How many times have I said not to use the ball in the house? Stop. Can you stop? You're going to mark the paint. You're marking the paint. Girls, are you going to eat these eggs? I've got a nice breakfast. Get out of the bathroom, for the love of God.

JOHN wanders off stage. We hear the noise of the basketball recede. HELEN continues giving instructions as though the children were at the table. And it begins to snow on her in the middle of the kitchen. Snow accumulates on her hair and bare shoulders and she's cold but she keeps beating the eggs, unaware of the snow.

Do you want to crack the legs off that chair? Don't lean back on the chair. Have you got your homework? Where's your shoe? Your other shoe. If you put your shoes in your bag after school we wouldn't have this problem. There's a nice hot bath for you. Well tell her to hurry up. Get out of the bathroom, Cathy. Your brother has to go. Who left the water all over the floor? Somebody clean up that water. Don't lean back on the— You're going to crack the legs off it. Eat your eggs. Just eat them, will you. Will you just— Eat the goddamn eggs. They're threatening to cut off the heat. This is the third disconnection notice. I just can't remember to pay it. You've got basketball practice after school. I've got a nice breakfast for you. Your breakfast is nice and hot, come and get it while it's hot. These are nice fresh eggs. Brown eggs. Okay, brush your teeth. Are they brushed? Did you brush your teeth? Scrape your plate. Hey, get back here. Put it in the sink. What do you think I am, your personal slave? Good boy, I love you. You didn't eat your eggs. There's a Flakie in your lunch. Don't blame me if every tooth you have rots right out of your head. I love you. Do you know that? Have I ever told you that before? That I love you more than life itself. Have a great day, okay? I love you. Have a really great— Mommy loves you. I love you.

The kettle whistles shrilly and HELEN puts down the bowl of eggs and the whisk and covers her ears.

SCENE XVIII

Lights down and they come up on an office. There's a man standing facing a window with his back to the door. JOHN knocks and enters.

RED: Ronnie McPherson.

JOHN: Ronnie. John O'Mara.

RED: Red.

JOHN: Pardon, sir?

RED: Call me Red.

JOHN: Okay, sir. Red.

RED: Just Red.

JOHN: Pardon, sir?

RED: Not sir, just Red.

JOHN: Sorry. Red. Is it because…? Because you're not a redhead, are you?

RED: It stuck. That's all.

JOHN: Sure. Red.

RED: You come recommended. Let's see, you began…?

JOHN: I started crawling into petroleum tanks checking for fissures and cracks.

RED: You crawled in there with equipment?

He's leafing through a folder that contains JOHN's resumé.

JOHN: Ultrasound equipment. Checking for cracks, fissures, anything that's going to—

RED: Cost.

JOHN: Leak.

RED: How'd you like that?

JOHN: It was a squeeze. It was a tight squeeze in there. Very dark. I mean black. It was pitch black in there. They tied ropes to my ankles is what they did, and if I got into trouble they could haul me out.

RED: You were a kid?

JOHN: Nineteen, twenty.

RED: And then you?

JOHN: I've done pretty much everything from there. Covered every aspect of the industry, basically. Engineering, of course.

RED: You've got a few degrees there. Engineering degree, I see.

JOHN: And communications.

RED: Another degree. I don't put much stock in degrees, John. I'll tell you that up front. The industry doesn't put much stock in formal education. We're like the military. We like to train our own. I got a grade nine education.

JOHN: I've been out on the rigs. I've done image-consulting, risk-assessment, I've been all over. Nigeria, Scotland, Sudan, Middle East.

RED: You get around.

JOHN: Then I got your call.

RED: Look, we're an independent arm here at Shoreline, John. Impartial. That gives us a lot of freedom. We speak to government; we speak to industry; we liaise; we're global in reach.

JOHN: I understand that.

RED: We're looking for someone like you, John. Someone who knows all the aspects of the industry. From the floor up. Someone who can hold sway whether he's in a boardroom or on the deck of a rig. Young, bright, lots of energy. A company like this we need a guy understands the optics.

JOHN: I think I can bring a lens to this thing. I think I can articulate, if you give me a chance, the company behind the brand, the philosophy.

RED: There's a culture out there, see, John, that doesn't understand the notion of risk, or efficiency.

JOHN: You're talking image. Optics. And I have ideas.

RED: I know you do. I've heard. Frankly there's a culture of safety out there right now that's got a stranglehold on innovation, on profit management. Then there's us guys, guys with vision. There's no room in this industry for little old ladies. We're a company that has to think of its stakeholders; we have to think of the public good. This is an industry—we're looking to trim.

JOHN: Trim?

RED: Absolutely. That's another word for efficiency, John. Trim, shave, cut. These are all words. You spend enough time with me you'll see that efficiency's my favourite word. Say it for me.

JOHN: Mr. McPherson.

RED: Red.

Say it for me. Then I'm going to make you an offer, John. And I think it's one you're going to like. I think you'll like it very much.

RED scribbles the offer on a piece of paper, folds it, slides it across the desk.

You're going to like this offer.

JOHN: Efficiency.

RED: I understand you lost your father on the *Ocean Ranger*, John.

RED holds his finger on the paper.

JOHN: Yes, my father died on the *Ocean Ranger*.

He lets JOHN take up the paper.

RED: I was sorry to hear that. I hope that's not going to affect your judgment when difficult decisions arise.

JOHN: I don't think so, sir. If anything I think that experience will enable me... to go forward.

RED: This figure is what you'd start with. We'll want you in two weeks. You'll go through training, we show you the ropes, the ins and outs, you'll meet your staff. You'll have to refresh your safety course.

JOHN: Safety course? The simulated helicopter in the swimming pool?

RED: Everybody does the safety course, John. That's optics.

Lights down.

SCENE IXX

LOUISE has shown up with groceries that she's putting away in HELEN's cupboards. The lighting changes to let us know we have returned to 1982. Ten-year-old JOHN is hanging around the kitchen table, waiting to see if there are any treats.

HELEN: My God, Louise.

LOUISE: I know, honey, you're my baby sister.

HELEN: You shouldn't have to do this.

JOHN: What did Aunt Lou do?

HELEN: She bought our groceries. She and Uncle Frank. They're helping us out, Johnny.

LOUISE: This is: don't even mention it. Don't bring it up. Look what I have!

JOHN: Pop-Tarts!

HELEN: Not before dinner you don't.

LOUISE: Oh let him, Helen. You promise to eat your dinner, don't you, honey?

HELEN: You can't afford this any more than me, Louise.

LOUISE: Don't be so foolish.

HELEN: I'll have money soon. I'll pay you back. It's just taking so bloody long.

LOUISE: They're watching their asses is what. Go on now, Johnny, go on upstairs and eat your Pop-Tart. Get at your homework.

JOHN: Thanks, Aunt Lou.

He exits slowly, like he'd rather stay and listen to the adults.

LOUISE: Go on, I said.

She waits until he's gone.

So what's this about a phone call?

HELEN: His teacher. I had to go in. She says he's having difficulties. Apparently he chews on his pencils. He's eating them. She says he's going through a pencil a week, she figures. He just chews them down. God knows how much he's swallowing. She says it can't be good for him. And he's chewing on the cuffs of his shirt. The cuffs are soaking wet and threadbare when he gets home. And he sits alone at lunch. He's always alone. And there was an incident. They threw his shoes up in the tree. These boys did. And he was out there in the snow in his stocking feet.

LOUISE: They all do that. They all have something they do, Helen. He's sad; he lost his father. There's a lot of pressure.

HELEN: I depend on him, Louise, and he's only ten. I've got the girls. I'm exhausted. He's the one that gets up with Gabby. In the middle of the night. Gets a bottle for her. Sometimes we're all of us in the bed together. I haven't slept a night through since the rig went down. I don't think I'll ever sleep again.

LOUISE: This roast was on sale. You should have it this Sunday.

HELEN: It feels like I'm outside, Louise. Like all this is on the inside, these eggs, those spaghetti noodles, this *(referring to an unlabelled can)* whatever this is. All of this is on the inside and I'm outside, you know what I mean? I watch myself. It's like going to the theatre. It's like tapping on a glass. Looking at my own reflection. I'm buttering the toast, but I'm watching myself buttering the toast. I fold the laundry, and my hands are going, here's one sock, and here's the other. That's what people do. And then you have a pile of socks and it looks like you're on the inside. But there's an outside, Louise. I didn't know about. I'm way out there. I'm in outer space. And it's cold out here, let me tell you. I can't let the kids know about it. I do everything now so the kids won't know, it's so they'll think I'm on the inside with them. But Johnny knows. He knows.

SCENE XX

HELEN is getting dressed on stage. It's 2009 and she's looking in a full-length mirror, putting on cocktail dress, brushing her hair, getting ready to apply makeup. CAL is sitting in an armchair facing the audience.

HELEN: You know what the worst part of running into you would be? I think this might be the worst part if I ran into you. You'd still be young.

CAL: You're young, Helen.

HELEN: It went by in a minute. Sometimes I look in the mirror and I just think, that's not me. I *feel* twenty-five. Of course, everybody says that. Everybody. It all happened so fast. Like I wasn't there for it, or something. Or I was there for it. I was there for it, right in the middle of it, so I missed it going past. I didn't stand back and take stock. Who's counting, right? There was no time for counting.

She looks at herself in the mirror.

I feel like I'm a thousand years old.

CAL: You've changed.

HELEN: The kids changed me.

CAL: I know, the kids.

HELEN: You have no idea.

CAL: I couldn't know.

HELEN: I felt abandoned. That was it. It was like you left.

CAL: We weren't trained.

HELEN: I know.

CAL: We didn't stand a chance.

HELEN: I read the report. Believe me. I got that thing memorized.

CAL: They didn't train us. They said read the manual. Nobody read the manual. And a list developed.

HELEN: Everybody was so desperate for work. We had a little baby coming. When I think of it. We were so young.

Beat.

What happened to you? That's what I want to know. Where were you when that thing started to go down?

HELEN gets up and crosses the stage to him. She kneels down in front of him and puts her hand on his cheek.

CAL: You think you want to know this. What happened out there. You don't want to know.

HELEN: Your skin is so smooth, Cal. You're beautiful. A very handsome guy. You were hot. God, I felt so lucky.

CAL: We heard the alarm but we ignored it. The b'ys had towels plugging up the speakers so they could sleep.

HELEN: I woke up and it was like you were in the bathroom, brushing your teeth. I could hear you. Just the ordinary sounds. I heard the lid to the garbage bucket hit the wall. You step on the little pedal and the lid flies up, I heard that. And the water running. I heard all that plain as day and you said come look out the window. And I got up and looked, but you weren't there.

CAL: It wasn't a surprise, Helen. Everybody knew all along. We knew from day one. But to tell you the truth, Helen, we didn't think the rig. What we thought was the helicopters. Scared shitless of the helicopters. Those things. They're not maintained, we knew that. We knew we were taking our lives in our hands.

HELEN: You get shy is what happens. You get crippled by shyness. The most frightening thing is you get used to it. And you get used to not having sex. You get used to not being touched. What a fright when you realize what you're after getting used to. You realize how long it's been since somebody touched you. I'm just talking ordinary human contact. Somebody brushing away a bit of lint, or your shoulders touching in a crowded elevator. Pretty soon you don't miss it. You miss something, but you can't put your finger on what it is. The idea of taking off my clothes. I mean if I was to meet somebody. You have no idea. It's not like when you're twenty. Or twenty-five. You never should have been out there. But at the time. Remember when you got the job? Jesus, Cal.

CAL: I had a family. I had to be out there.

HELEN: I mean I'm still in shape. Sort of. I'm doing yoga. I hope I never have to look another Lean Cuisine in the face, I tell you that.

CAL: What are you getting dressed up for?

HELEN: I don't know. I have a date. I'm trying to get out there, you know what I mean? Get out there, be really bright and witty. Upbeat. I feel guilty. I still feel guilty, isn't that something? The thing is, you haven't gone through it all. You left me. That's what happened, Cal. You left me. I was left alone. You stopped but I didn't stop.

She stands up and goes back to her vanity table to finish her makeup.

I used to just want to walk right out into the ocean. When it was snowing. Take off all my clothes and walk out into it just to see what it would have felt like. Sometimes I still want that. I had to do everything by myself and you were so young. You were so young. That's the thing, way too young. Nothing else happened to you. And look at me now. I'm old. If we met on the beach, say a beach in Greece or something like that, I'd just be this old woman. One of those old women you see on the beach, with the bathing suits with the little pleated skirts to cover the dimply thighs. I have age spots. I mean, they're not very big or anything. I only have two. I mean they're more like freckles, I s'pose. Big freckles. But I'd be one of those women, an older woman, and you'd be the way you were twenty-seven years ago.

SCENE XXI

HELEN leaves the bedroom and goes into the living room where BARRY is working.

BARRY: You look nice.

HELEN: Thank you.

BARRY: Special occasion?

He is measuring a piece of wood, drawing lines with a pencil. HELEN is putting in her earrings.

HELEN: Yes, actually. I have a date.

BARRY: Well.

HELEN: You're surprised.

BARRY: No, no, not at all. No. Have a good time.

HELEN: I will. Can you lock up when you leave?

BARRY: Sure. It's cold out there.

HELEN: I'll be fine.

The door closes and BARRY gives a chair a kick.

SCENE XXII

The lights go down and come up with the echoey sounds of a swimming pool. There are four men in scuba gear, presumably underwater. In the soundscape we hear the noise of their breathing through the mouthpieces of their oxygen tanks. There's a chair in the centre of the stage that has straps over it. The straps are the same harness we saw earlier in the zipline scene. A video screen full of ocean waves. We hear the noise of a hydraulic winch and the simulated helicopter rises from the bottom of the pool. The sound of water sloshing off it.

COACH: I'm looking for a volunteer to go first. Let's see, O'Mara, John.

JOHN: I didn't volunteer, sir.

COACH: On my record here it shows you've failed this part of the test five times, O'Mara.

JOHN: I have a phobia, sir.

COACH: What's that, son?

JOHN: Of putting my face in water. I don't like water on my face. Ever since I was a kid. My father drowned. I can't stand it. I don't like being submerged.

COACH: You're going to have to get over it, O'Mara. I see you've been picked up by Shoreline. Congratulations, young man. Image consultant. Here's an image for you, O'Mara. The image is a helicopter goes down in the North Atlantic and men and women are trained to evacuate. Got that?

JOHN: Thank you, sir. I wonder if there's a way we could overlook this section of the training program in my case.

COACH: Listen, O'Mara, do you know how many men have died out there because safety was overlooked? The last time you were here you passed out cold.

JOHN: I nearly died down there, sir.

COACH: There's nothing to worry about, O'Mara. We've got four men down there in wetsuits. You just kick open the door and fling it aside, undo your seatbelt, and swim up to the surface. If there's any trouble we've got a team there to get you to the surface, get you breathing again. Now. Are you ready?

Stage right, JOHN sits down in the chair and is strapped in. He's given a plastic door to hold on to. The door is attached to invisible strings and when JOHN throws it aside it will float to the surface. The chair tips over with JOHN still strapped to it. He begins to panic; he can't get the seatbelt undone. The sound of him thrashing in the pool. Splashes, reverberations. We hear a voice-over of the S.O.S. sent from the rig. The voices of the men from the Ocean Ranger *calling for backup. Calling for helicopters. Send everything you have. The sounds of the pool turn slowing into the sounds of a gale-force storm, raging waves. HELEN comes out onto stage left and snow begins to fall on her. She's standing in a spotlight. She's shouting over the storm. The COACH crosses over from the simulated helicopter scene into HELEN's side of the stage. He has become one of the sailors on the deck of the* Seaforth Highlander. *He is battling the wind to answer her.*

HELEN: Where is he? Is he in the water? Where is he? Did you see him?

COACH: There were a lot of men in the water. There wasn't very much time, Helen. We were trying to get to them.

CAL walks down the centre of the stage between the training scene with JOHN and the scene with HELEN and the sailor. He is speaking to the audience. HELEN and the COACH cannot see him.

CAL: There was a dead calm on the rig. That was the strange thing. Someone said, "Get in here and clean up this glass." Somebody said, "The panel is wet." "Valves opening by themselves," somebody said. "Get down here and get it cleaned up."

HELEN: What did he say? Did Cal say anything? Did he say my name? Did he call out for me?

COACH: The ropes were iced over, you could hardly hear. The wind took a metal shed off one of the vessels. It just blew off. The decks were iced over, our faces, our hands, we were trying to reach out to them. You could see them there but it was so bloody cold. They couldn't raise their arms to grab a hold to anything. We couldn't get to them, see, Helen. We couldn't get close enough to 'em.

CAL: *(to audience)* There was smoke. There were blue sparks. The PA system died. We were running for the lifeboats, and you could feel the whole thing tipping. Someone said, "Send the helicopters." They said, "Send everything you have."

HELEN: Did he call out that he loved me, or that he'd miss us, or anything? Did he have any idea about the baby? I wanted him to have an intuition about the baby. I wanted him to know there was a baby coming.

CAL: *(to audience)* We sent out the mayday. "We have a list from which we cannot recover." That's what the mayday said. "Send everything you have." The lifeboats destroyed, some of them, soon as they hit the water.

COACH: We were yelling out to them. We wanted them to hear a human voice, that's what we were trying to do. That's all we could do. Yell to them so they'd know they weren't alone.

HELEN: He didn't say anything. He must have been so alone out there. He was so alone.

Lights out on everyone but CAL. *Sound effects silenced.*

CAL: You want to know what it was like? This is the true account of what it was like out there the night the rig went down. There was a crevasse in the wave. I don't know what it was. It was a wave of concrete or it was glass. And the wave opened up to let us in. Trying to hang on to the rail but the rail was iced over. You looked into it and you knew, this wall of water had always existed. It did not design itself or come into being or form. There was never a forming of. It just is. It is still and self-combusting. Full of mystery, full of void. Full of God. Get down on your knees before this creature. It is the centre of the outside. This wave is death. When we say death we mean something we cannot say. The wave—because it is just water, after all, just water, just naked power, just force—the wave is the mirror image of death, not death itself, but it's to your advantage not to glance that way. Avoid the mirror if you can. But the thing is, death would like to be introduced. It's willing to be polite. There's no rush. And listen, when it closed over me it seemed like life had been a dalliance, a moment. There and gone. Because since the beginning of time this wave had been working towards the chewing and swallowing of the world. What is the world, after all? What is sunlight and love and the birth of a child and all the small passions that break out and flare and matter so very much? A great big guzzling of itself is death, or what the end of life may be called, or referred to as, or spoken of. We don't know how to name it because it is unknowable. Except now I know it. I know it. It is a glittering thing, big and disco-ball beautiful, full of dazzle, and I left her for it. I was swallowed whole.

JOHN is flat on his back. He coughs, spews a mouthful of water. Slams his hand on the floor. Gasps for breath. He's shaking, cold, traumatized.

JOHN: You nearly killed me. Do you understand that? I could have drowned down there. Jesus Christ. Image management. If one these things goes down you don't have a chance in hell. That's the image. They aren't safe. Those helicopters aren't safe. You nearly killed me. Manage that, you bastards, manage that.

In the middle of JOHN's rant he starts working his way out of the safety suit and once it is off he stands alone. Everyone else has left the stage. He kicks impotently at the harness he has struggled out of in the last throes of rage. He finds his phone. He tips it and water drips out, but miraculously it works. He is amazed by it, amazed that it has survived the water. He dials a number.

Oh. Hi. Don't hang up. I'm sorry, okay? Wait. Are you there? I'm sorry. Listen. You kind of took me by surprise. Of course not. I know, I was an asshole. I know that. Absolutely. You did the right thing. Thank you. You know. Thank you for calling. I've been thinking. And you know, my first reaction. That's not a real indication. I think we need to sit down or something. I'm home now. Back from Tasmania. It was something. It was. It's wasn't Iceland. I mean the food wasn't. But it was good. I did this thing. A zipline. You just stand on the edge of a cliff and you drop, like a hundred feet. You just let yourself fall. Give into it; it's incredible. But, yeah, never mind. Okay, listen. Could we meet? I could take you out to dinner. What about Tuesday? Oh jeez, I forgot it's New Year's Eve… I just think we need to sit down, talk about this thing, what do you say?

SCENE XXIII

We return to the scene in the bedroom where HELEN *is preparing for a date.* CAL *is sitting in the armchair watching her. She's putting on makeup now.*

HELEN: Laugh lines. That's what those are. If I'd been more of a sourpuss my whole life I wouldn't have this problem right now.

CAL: You got a date?

HELEN: It's New Year's Eve. Yes, I have a date.

CAL: Who is it?

HELEN: I don't know. I don't know who he is. How can you know? The thing is I feel something. For the first time.

CAL: You're alive. That's the thing. You're alive.

HELEN: It's completely silly. I've cooked this meal. I must of taken the candles off the table three times. Take them off, put them back on. I don't know. Candles? I feel like I know him.

CAL: I like your laugh lines. I think they're sexy.

HELEN: I mean why the hell not, right? If I want candles on New Year's Eve. The gravy. You know what my gravy is like. I don't know. It's not about the food, right?

CAL: Look out the window, Helen. There's people all over the city heading out for parties. I think I'll go outside. Take in the fireworks.

HELEN *looks at her watch. There's the sound of the doorbell.*

HELEN: Oh my God, he's here. He's here. Do I look okay? Well, it's as good as it's going to get.

She's checking her bum in the mirror. Seemingly she has forgotten about CAL.

CAL *leaves the stage and* HELEN *leaves the bedroom to go down and answer the door but she stops suddenly and returns to the vanity table and removes her wedding ring and leaves it there.*

SCENE XXIV

The sound and light of fireworks bursts all over the stage in a video, "Auld Lang Syne." The stage is split in two. Ordinary stage lights rise on two tables, one in a hotel restaurant, the other in HELEN's dining room. JOHN is sitting at one, the hotel restaurant table. He's turning his knife end over end. He's very agitated, checking his watch. At the same time BARRY is sitting at the other table. He's still in his carpenter outfit, though it's New Year's Eve. He is tucking into a whole plate of food, has it all gobbled down by the time HELEN shows up on stage. She is dressed up in a beautiful evening dress and has her own plate of food. She sees he's eaten his before she's even had a chance to sit down and she's disappointed. On the opposite side of the stage JOHN drops his knife and it clatters to the floor. He picks it up and when he sits up there is a very pregnant woman standing in front of him. Sometimes the talking from both tables overlaps, particularly when the characters are saying some of the same words or lines.

JOHN: My God, you're big. Beautiful. You're beautiful.

He jumps up to hug her but he's afraid he will hurt her belly. He moves very gingerly and ends up just patting her on the arm. Then they move in for a kiss and knock foreheads.

JANE: It's good to see you.

He pulls up a chair for her.

JOHN: Hey, you bet. Yes, sir. Yes.

JANE: I guess I've changed. It's a bit of a shock? And I'm late. I fell asleep in the chair in the hotel room. Fell asleep sitting up. I fall asleep all the time now. I've kept you waiting.

HELEN: No, no that's fine. You go ahead.

BARRY: I should have waited for you.

JOHN: No, I haven't been waiting.

HELEN: I didn't want it to get cold.

BARRY: It just smelled so good.

BARRY jumps up to pull out HELEN's chair at the same time that JOHN jumps up to pull out the chair for JANE.

HELEN: You know what? I'm sorry, the gravy's all congealed; it's a disaster. Look at it.

BARRY: Could I have seconds?

JOHN: You should have a drink. A Scotch. A nice stiff Scotch.

JANE: Water for me, please.

JOHN: Oh, sorry, right. Excuse me, could we get a second glass of water over here?

HELEN: You want seconds?

BARRY: Sure.

HELEN: Listen, I don't know what I was thinking. I heard you on your cellphone.

JANE: I found your cellphone number on a scrap of paper.

JOHN: I don't know what I was thinking. You took me by surprise. A baby.

BARRY: What do you mean? You heard a phone call?

JANE: I had to call. That's the truth of it. I had to tell you, that's what it came down to.

HELEN: Talking to someone you love. I heard you say "I love you." I wasn't listening, I just heard it. You were going to pick someone up after work, you said, "I love you." I'd like to know. If you have someone. I feel like I have a right to know. Because. I think something is going on here.

JANE: I'm not sure what I'm doing here.

HELEN: I'm just not sure what I'm doing here, if you're married, or if you have someone.

JANE: I don't want to marry you or anything. It isn't about you and me.

BARRY: It was a child.

HELEN: It was a child?

BARRY: My grandchild.

JANE: We're talking about a child here, John.

HELEN: It was a child? On the phone. You have a grandchild?

BARRY: My daughter's girl. I was picking her up from school. I'm not with my wife anymore. It was a short-lived thing, just out of high school. That was a long time ago.

JANE: I know it was this really short-lived thing, but you have a right to know.

HELEN: I'm glad I know that. I just wanted to know.

JOHN: I'm glad I know.

JANE: I was going to stay with my father, but he has his own troubles, anyway; he's not supportive. He hung up on me when I called.

HELEN: So you're not with anyone?

JANE: I don't have anyone right now.

BARRY: I don't have anyone right now.

JOHN: We're going to figure this thing out, Jane. I don't know what kind of thing we'll work out. But you don't have to go through this alone. I'm saying. Whatever you want.

BARRY lights the candle.

BARRY: Let me light the candles here, Helen. Let's have a little candlelight.

HELEN: Oh, that would be very nice.

JANE: I just need someone to be nice to me right now. I'm having a baby.

The sound of fireworks can be heard overlaid with the sound effects of a birthing room in a hospital. JANE goes behind the same curtain that HELEN was behind when she gave birth. Once again we see the birth occurring in shadow behind the curtain with all the doctors and nurses in attendance. While the baby is being born, this time, silently, HELEN and JOHN pull the chairs to the front of the stage. The video of the fireworks plays over the white curtain, behind which the baby is born. They sit down and face the audience again.

JOHN: We have a little girl. It's a girl. We have a little girl.

HELEN: I was just a girl. Just a girl. They didn't have the word "closure" back then. What a word. I was never looking for it. Don't go looking for that.

JOHN: Obviously we can't live together. We hardly know each other. But for the first few weeks.

HELEN: We spent the first few weeks after the wedding in Mexico, a honeymoon. The girls said Mexico. And I was on the beach and he was swimming out, the rough tides they have down there.

JOHN: It was rough, I mean her milk wouldn't come in and the stitches and the spring, then, sticking up out of her couch.

HELEN: That's where I was, on the shore.

JOHN: *(in unison)* That's where I was, on the couch.

HELEN: And a parasailer went over, flew over me, a man in a sling or whatever with the giant kites. They were offering rides.

JOHN: Quite a ride, the first few weeks, the little fists, and when I covered her eyes with my hand, the first moment, in the hospital, still slippery with all the guck, she was, and I covered her eyes, to make a shadow from the lights they had there, and she opened them.

HELEN: This thing was landing, farther down the beach, and there was a shadow, floated over me, I mean the chill. A shadow in all that light.

JOHN: And I looked up and Jane was, well, she'd broken some blood vessels in her cheeks from pushing, but we looked at each other, you know what I mean? Her eyes. We won't live together, we hardly know each other.

HELEN: There won't be anything like closure. Not ever. But I've known him. I have that.

JOHN: But we know each other. Sometimes things stay open.

HELEN: And I'm open. Wide open.

THE END

CONTRIBUTORS

ROBERT CHAFE is a playwright based in St. John's, Newfoundland, whose work has been seen across Canada, the UK, Australia, and in the United States. He is the author of numerous plays, including *Afterimage*, which won the Governor General's Literary Award for Drama in 2010; *Butler's Marsh* and *Tempting Providence*, which were shortlisted in 2004 for the Governor General's Literary Award for Drama; and *Under Wraps*. Robert currently works as artistic director and playwright for Artistic Fraud.

AIDEN FLYNN is an actor, director, and arts administrator from St. John's, NL. A graduate of MUN, he was the co-founder of the Shakespeare by the Sea Festival in 1993 and was also the founder of a number of other theatre-based ventures after leaving school. After eight years in Calgary, Aiden founded the Rabbittown Theatre Company in 2004. While at Rabbittown Theatre, Flynn also co-founded the New World Theatre Project in Cupids, which saw the construction of a replica Jacobean-style playhouse. Currently, he is Director of Newfoundland and Labrador's Arts and Culture Centres. He and his wife Sarah have a beautiful little girl, Evelyn Belle.

ANDY JONES has been a professional writer and actor for over forty years. He has written five critically acclaimed one-man comedy shows: *Out of the Bin*, *Still Alive*, *King O' Fun*, *To The Wall*, and *An Evening with Uncle Val*. He is well known as one of the members of the groundbreaking Newfoundland comedy troupe CODCO, in both its theatrical and television incarnations. Andy's numerous awards include two Gemini awards, election to the Newfoundland Arts Council Hall of Honour, the Newfoundland and Labrador Arts Council's BMO Winterset Award, Best Performance at the Atlantic Film Festival in Halifax, and the ACTRA Award of Excellence for Lifetime Achievement.

DR. DENYSE LYNDE is a professor in the English Department at Memorial University of Newfoundland, specializing in Canadian and Newfoundland drama. Her work has been published with Playwrights Canada Press, in *Canadian Theatre Review*, and in numerous other academic journals and newspapers.

LISA MOORE is the acclaimed author of *February*, which was longlisted for the Man Booker Prize, selected as one of *The New Yorker*'s Best Books of the Year, and was a *Globe and Mail* Top 100 Book; and *Alligator*, which was a finalist for the Scotiabank Giller Prize and won the Commonwealth Fiction Prize (Canada and the Caribbean), and was a national bestseller. Her story collection *Open* was a finalist for the Scotiabank Giller Prize and a national bestseller. Her third novel, *Caught*, was shortlisted for the Rogers Writers' Trust Fiction Prize and the Scotiabank Giller Prize and selected as an Amazon.ca Best Book. She lives in St. John's, Newfoundland.

EDWARD RICHE writes for the page, stage, and screen. His latest play for the Resource Centre for the Arts is *Dedication*. His latest novel is *Today I Learned It Was You*, published by House of Anansi Press in 2016. He lives in St. John's.

BERNI STAPLETON is a playwright, author, and director of unique distinction. She works to explore the inner lives of Newfoundlanders who find the extraordinary within the ordinary. She is a recent recipient of the Rhonda Payne Theatre Award from ArtsNL. She is a past recipient of the WANL award for best work in non-fiction for her book *They Let Down Baskets*. Her new book of short stories *This is the Cat* from Creative Books is winning rave reviews. She was recently featured in the prestigious *Cuffer Anthology* of short stories, and has been published in the anthologies *Voices From the Landwash* and *Going it Alone* and in the *Capilano Review*. She has been a regular contributor to *The Newfoundland Quarterly* and has been featured in *Riddle Fence*. You can find out more about Berni by visiting bernistapleton.com.